ACT Aspire
Grade 8
Reading/English/
Writing
SUCCESS STRATEGIES

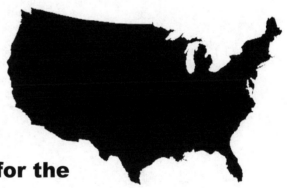

**ACT Aspire Test Review for the
ACT Aspire Assessments**

Dear Future Exam Success Story:

Congratulations on your purchase of our study guide. Our goal in writing our study guide was to cover the content on the test, as well as provide insight into typical test taking mistakes and how to overcome them.

Standardized tests are a key component of being successful, which only increases the importance of doing well in the high-pressure high-stakes environment of test day. How well you do on this test will have a significant impact on your future, and we have the research and practical advice to help you execute on test day.

The product you're reading now is designed to exploit weaknesses in the test itself, and help you avoid the most common errors test takers frequently make.

How to use this study guide

We don't want to waste your time. Our study guide is fast-paced and fluff-free. We suggest going through it a number of times, as repetition is an important part of learning new information and concepts.

First, read through the study guide completely to get a feel for the content and organization. Read the general success strategies first, and then proceed to the content sections. Each tip has been carefully selected for its effectiveness.

Second, read through the study guide again, and take notes in the margins and highlight those sections where you may have a particular weakness.

Finally, bring the manual with you on test day and study it before the exam begins.

Your success is our success

We would be delighted to hear about your success. Send us an email and tell us your story. Thanks for your business and we wish you continued success.

Sincerely,

Mometrix Test Preparation Team

Need more help? Check out our flashcards at:
http://MometrixFlashcards.com/ACTAspire

TABLE OF CONTENTS

Reading

Literature

Explicit information

Explicit information is the information that is found in a passage or story. This information can include facts, descriptions, and statements about the characters, setting, or events in a story. Explicit information is not suggested or hinted at; it is definite because it is stated right in the passage. Explicit information takes many shapes; in a description it might be that "Tom was taller than his brother." In dialogue it could be, "I have never been to Texas before." Or it could be found in an event: "Charles hit his head on the bottom of the swimming pool." Explicit information is often used as supporting evidence when making an inference.

Identify the explicit information in the following excerpt:

> Bernard loved to paint. He regularly worked eight hours a day, six days a week, perfecting his craft. His sister Julie was an actress. On days when she was performing or rehearsing, she put in very long hours. Sometimes she worked 14 or 16 hours a day.

Explicit information is information which is found within the text itself. It is not suggested in any way. This excerpt tells about a brother and sister and what they did. It tells us that Bernard loved to paint and worked on his painting eight hours a day. It also says that his sister Julie was an actress and that he sometimes rehearsed 14 or 16 hours a day. This information is all explicit. It is stated in the excerpt. The reader does not need to make an inference or guess at anything. Everything is factual. When you read, think about the information in the story and whether it is explicit or not.

Inference

An *inference* is basically a good guess that a reader makes using the explicit information that is in a passage or story. An inference can also be based on personal experience combined with the information in a passage. For instance, a story may say that several people are leaving a movie theater and many of them are crying. The logical conclusion, both from the explicit information and personal knowledge, is that the movie was sad. A good inference is supported by the information in a passage. Inferences are different from explicit information: they are not clearly stated in a passage, only hinted at. The reader must determine—or *infer*—for himself what the author is suggesting. A good reader puts the clues together to produce a conclusion that is both logical and likely to be true.

Read the following excerpt and decide why Alex did not want to see the puppy:

> Dr. Thomas walked up to Alex in the waiting room. He spoke as gently as he could. "I'm sorry about Rover. We did everything we could to save him. But he was just too sick. I know how much you loved him. But I have something to show you." Then Dr. Thomas showed Alex a cute little puppy. "No," the boy shouted. "I don't want to see your dog."

You can infer that Alex did not want to see the puppy because he was too upset about his own dog. This conclusion might be based both on what the passage says and from personal experience. In the excerpt, Dr. Thomas tells Alex that they could not save his dog. From personal experience you might realize how upsetting it is to lose a pet. That would help you come to the conclusion that Alex was grieving and didn't want to see another dog at that moment. An inference is based on the information in a passage and a reader's experience, but it is not stated in the text.

Determining the theme of a story

The *theme* of a story is the lesson that it teaches. It is what the reader learns from what happens in a story. The theme is linked to the characters, the setting, and the events in a story. The theme develops with the development of the plot. Some themes are fairly common. These themes are called *universal themes*; they suggest things about life, society, and human nature. Themes are an important part of literature because they serve the purpose of teaching the reader or listener a truth about life. The theme is developed by how a character or characters respond to their situations and challenges.

Tell why the theme of the following excerpt should be "Overconfidence can lead to a fall:"

> Bella was happy. She auditioned for the starring role in the school play and she felt sure she'd got the part. Afterwards, she told her friends she would be starring in the play. But on Tuesday when the director said they had offered the part to Sara Goodwin, she started crying.

The excerpt tells the story of a girl who has an audition and thinks she got the starring role. She is so confident that she even tells her friends that she has the part. But then she learns that the role was offered to someone else and she starts to cry. She was overly confident about her success and was subsequently devastated when she learned of her failure, and that is the lesson of the story. If you are overly confident you may have a fall. That is the theme of the story. A theme is the lesson that a story teaches. This particular theme is found often in literature. A theme is not stated in a passage: the reader must deduce it from the plot of the story.

Objective summary

An *objective summary* of a story has several components. It should include the main idea of the story, the most important details or events that occur, and the main characters and what happens to them. A summary is not a general statement about what a story is about, nor is it a paraphrase. Paraphrases retell a story and give too much information about what happens, including some that is not important; summaries do not. A summary will not include everything in the story. In order to write an objective summary, you will need to think about what happens in the story. You will need to decide what it is mostly about and what details are the most important. Objective summaries do not include personal feelings or opinions.

Read the summary and discuss how it could be improved:

> This story is about a man and a woman who moved to the West many years ago. There was a lot of information about covered wagons or "prairie schooners," as they called them. I liked the story because of that.

The summary tells the main idea of the story, but it doesn't include the details of what happens in the story. It does not include the main characters and what they did or what challenges they faced. It does not summarize the plot. Another problem with the summary is that it is not objective; it is subjective. The writer describes what he thinks about the story. But personal opinions have no place in an objective summary of a story. To improve it, the writer should remove his personal opinion and add descriptions of who was in the story, what important things happened to them, and how the story ended.

Driving the action

There are many ways in which the action of a story may be driven. Dialogue is one of them. What a character says either to another character or about a situation may propel the action by revealing what a character is thinking or what he may do. Similarly, what a character says will tell the audience what he is like. His manner of speaking, what he says, and how he says it are all clues to his personality. Dialogue can also provoke a decision by showing what the character intends to do in the future. Incidents in a story also propel the action because the plot is made up of events that build on events. Incidents such as a confrontation could reveal aspects of a character or provoke a decision.

Read the excerpt and tell how it reveals aspects of the speaker:

> I told you I wasn't ever going to become a doctor and yet here you are bringing the topic up again. I think I am just going to put a sign on my door that says "No Medical School." Are you going to harangue me all day?

The person who is speaking sounds very sure of what he does not want to do and is forcefully resisting any attempt by someone else, a person not revealed, to try to get him to go to medical school. The speaker's character is resolute and somewhat dramatic because he plans to put a sign on his door to remind the unnamed person that he has no intention of doing what the other person wants. It could be a parent, a wife or even a friend who is urging this action. The character also seems somewhat young because he seems to have to defend his decision so strongly.

Read the excerpt and tell how this incident propels the action of the story and provokes a decision:

> It was a perfect day it seemed, until Sam saw the thunderheads roll in. He knew that it would be dangerous to be in a rowboat in the middle of the lake during a thunder and lightning storm. Suddenly the sky became darker and he heard a clap of thunder.

This incident certainly propels the action of the story. It would appear that Sam is in a rowboat in the middle of the lake having a lovely time when he hears a clap of thunder. He realizes that a lake is a dangerous place to be so this event means that Sam must take action. What that action is would be of interest to the reader because it will help form the plot of the story. The incident also forces Sam to make a decision about what he should do. This will help the reader better understand Sam as a character.

Context clues

Context clues are one of the best tools in understanding the meaning of unknown words or phrases. The sentence that contains the word or phrase and the sentences before and after the unknown word or phrase often have clues that suggest the meaning. When attempting to understand what a word or phrase means, try to think of a synonym and then replace the unknown word with the synonym to see if it makes sense in the sentence. Many words have more than one meaning, so it is only the context that will tell the reader what is meant. For instance, the word "bluff" can mean a trick or a kind of hill. In the sentence "He stood on a bluff overlooking the ocean," the context is clear. In this instance it means a type of hill.

Read the following sentences and tell how to understand the meaning of "sedentary:"

> I like my job typing medical records except for one thing. I find it very sedentary. I would rather have a job where I can move around more.

"Sedentary" means "inactive" or "deskbound." When you read the excerpt you can determine the meaning from the context clues. The selection tells you that the author likes his job except for one thing and that he would rather have a job that allowed him to move around more. This clue helps you understand what "sedentary" means. If you insert the synonyms "inactive" or "deskbound" in place of "sedentary," you can see that the excerpt makes sense. Context clues help you understand the meanings of unknown words. Context clues are hints as to the meaning of a word or phrase.

Figurative language

Figurative language is the use of words and expressions to expand reality in a vivid way. It is the use of language in a non-literal way, which means using language in a non-traditional manner in order to create an image. It is often used by poets. Examples of figurative language include simile, metaphor, personification, hyperbole, onomatopoeia and alliteration. *Similes* compare things using the words "like" or "as," for example, "She is as gentle as a lamb." *Metaphors* compare things without using comparing words: "She is a lamb when dealing with others." *Personification* gives a thing or animal human traits: "The ocean spoke of foreign places and dreams." *Hyperbole* is an exaggeration that is vivid but not believable: "She is the kindest person in the world." *Onomatopoeia* is when words sound like what they are, such as "hiss, hiss" to describe the sound a snake makes. *Alliteration* is the use of consecutive words that start with the same letter: "Raining, ripping, racing, running…"

Read the excerpt and tell what form of figurative language the phrase "come down like a sluggish sea" is and why:

> The weather changed. The air had come down like a sluggish sea, weighing us down with its heavy pressure.

The phrase, "air had come down like a sluggish sea" is an example of a simile. Similes add depth to writing and make it richer. They are used to create a more vivid image of something in the reader's mind. In this case, the air coming down "like a sluggish sea" means the air is very heavy. The phrase is not a metaphor because it compares to things using a comparison word, in this case "like." It can't be hyperbole as there is no exaggeration in the phrase. It is not an example of personification or onomatopoeia either, although there is a hint of alliteration in the phrase.

Denotative vs. connotative meaning of words

Words often have both a denotative meaning and a connotative meaning. The *denotative meaning* is the dictionary definition of a word. The *connotative meaning* is the associations that a word carries with it, associations above and beyond its literal meaning. For instance, the word "decorative" is a synonym for "fancy," but so is the word "extravagant." Yet "extravagant" has a rather negative meaning where "decorative" does not. "Extravagant" suggests something that is overdone or excessive. Readers should recognize the connotative meanings that writers include in their stories in order to better understand the writers' intent.

Read the following sentence and explain the connotative meanings of "strong-willed" and how it compares to "pig-headed:"

> Some people admired Uncle Fred because they thought he was strong-willed, but others considered him pig-headed.

Both the words "strong-willed" and "pig-headed" have the literal or denotative meaning of "stubborn." The word "pig-headed," however, also has a rather negative connotation of being so stubborn to the point of being stupid and that people are frustrated by such a person, while "strong-willed" has a more positive meaning of being stubborn as a good characteristic. The connotations that a word add to a sentence will influence how the reader interprets a story's characters and events. That is why it is important to notice which words the writer chooses to use. In this instance, the writer has drawn a contrast between positive and negative.

Read the excerpt and tell how the analogy impacts the tone of the story:

> Clara nestled underneath a tree, with her book, much in the same way that Alice of Wonderland fame might have done. Then, just like Alice, she fell asleep.

The words that a writer uses to tell a story are important because they can evoke a strong reaction in a reader. Here the writer makes an analogy to "Alice in Wonderland" in the way he describes Clara nestled under a tree with a book. The story of "Alice in Wonderland" is well known, and by making a reference to it, the writer creates a mood of mystery and tension about what may happen. The reader finds himself wondering if Clara will encounter some of the characters that Alice did when she says that Clara fell asleep. When reading, make sure to be aware of any analogy or references that the author makes to other texts to better comprehend what the author is suggesting.

Comparing and contrasting the structure of a poem to a short story

Poems have many structures. There are sonnets, haiku, and even pattern poems that take the shape of the focus of the poem. Poetry has developed over many years and its structure can be strict or, in the case of free verse, without rules. Generally a sonnet is a 14-line structure with a specific rhyming pattern and meter. Sonnets have been popular for a very long time and were a specialty of William Shakespeare. Haiku is a Japanese form of poetry that features three lines of five, seven, and five syllables, respectively. There are no strictures that are similar in a short story. Stories follow the order of the plot: the beginning, middle and end. But even that is not always the case with modern fiction, which may lack a real beginning or a definite end. Again the structure plays into the meaning and style of the poem or story by signaling to the reader the intent.

Dramatic irony

Dramatic irony is a situation when a character makes a remark about doing something that seems harmless in its context, but that the audience has more information about and realizes it could result in something unpleasant. This difference in knowledge can create suspense or humor depending on the circumstances. For instance, if a character says, "I will have a cup of tea now," and the audience knows that there is poison in the tea, it creates a situation that is suspenseful. That is an example of dramatic irony. The word "irony" comes from the Greek word for "dissembling" and it was used to describe what the Greeks thought was the gap between appearance and reality.

Transforming a story to a live performance

When transforming a story or drama to a live performance, either on stage or in film, a director will need to make decisions on how to present the story. Certainly the experience of seeing a performance of a story or drama is different because actors are speaking the dialogue or lines and are bringing the words and characters to life. But many directors choose to change the dialogue to simplify or emphasize a certain aspect of the play or film. Another decision that might be made in a staged performance is how the characters act; they may do something differently from what a person might imagine when reading a script. Yet another factor that might be different is the time period in which the action takes place. In particular, in both filmed and staged versions of Shakespearean plays, directors sometimes choose to bring the action into a modern world rather than keep it set in the time of the Renaissance.

How a filmed production of the story of Snow White might be different from the written story

In a filmed production of Snow White, you would see Snow White as a person who has certain traits that might be different from the written character. Also the evil stepmother might be better rendered and the reasons that she hated Snow White might be made clearer. Some directors might make the evil queen justified in her hatred of Snow White. For instance, a television series called "Once Upon a Time" presents these fairy tale characters in ways very different from the popular perception of them, giving reasons for their actions that were not included in the famous story.

How a modern fiction draws from the past

There is an old saying that writers like to quote: "there's nothing new under the sun." And to a large extent this is true because many of the modern stories, themes, patterns of events, and character types are taken from traditional stories, myths or religious works and then changed to make them seem new. For instance, the film "Wrath of the Titans," which is a sequel takes up where its predecessor, "Clash of the Titans," ended. These films are based on the myth of the ancient Greek hero Perseus and the tale of his life, which most people do not know. But that fact is unimportant because the movie makes the plot readily available to them. Mainstream actors give these mythic characters life, and the movies are filled with action to excite the audience by bringing an ancient tale to life while using the most advanced technology to create special effects. While the story is from myth, the director makes it current in that the actors bring color and personality to the mythic people they play.

Informational Texts

Finding textual evidence

Explicit information is information that is stated in a text. It is not something that is hinted at. A nonfiction text is usually made up of a main idea and supporting details. These supporting details are explicit: they are stated right in the text. They can be used to support an inference that is not stated in the text, or to support the main claims of an essay. Supporting information should be based on fact, not opinion. It should come from a reliable source and be something that others can verify. When trying to find textual evidence for what a text says explicitly, you will need to look for details that give more information about it.

Read the following excerpt and identify which information is explicit:

> In ancient times the value of an ox was the basis for the monetary systems of the Greeks, Assyrians, Mesopotamians, and the Egyptians. Each of these territories had their own currency. For instance, Egypt traded in gold and Greece in silver or copper.

All of the information in the excerpt is explicit. Nothing is hinted at. It says that the value of an ox was the basis for the monetary system for ancient Greeks, Assyrians, Mesopotamians, and the Egyptians. It adds that each of these territories had their own currency. It further informs that Egypt traded in gold and Greece in silver or copper. All of this information is factual. There are no opinions in the excerpt. There is nothing with which to make an inference. The details support the main idea that the ancients had monetary systems. All of the information can be checked to see if it is accurate.

Inference

An inference is a best guess. It is a conclusion that a reader can make from the information in a passage. For instance, if a passage says that a man is running down the street holding a woman's handbag, and there is a woman yelling for help in the distance, someone watching the scene might come up with the conclusion that the man is a thief and has stolen the woman's handbag. It could be an incorrect conclusion, but based on the evidence in the passage, it is the best guess that can be made. When you make an inference, you need to be able to tell what textual evidence supports the conclusion or inference. In this case, the fact that a man is running away holding a woman's handbag and a woman is yelling for help leads you to the conclusion.

Identify which information in the excerpt supports the inference that plants need more water when it is hot than when it is cool:

> Sweat is water that evaporates on the skin. Sweating is a process which cools the body. People sweat more in hot weather. Similarly, plants are cooled by evaporating water. Most of the water a plant takes in is used to keep it cool.

The information that supports the inference that plants need more water when it is hot then when it is cool is that plants are like people. The excerpt says that plants are cooled by evaporating water. The excerpt also says that people sweat more in hot weather, so the reader can determine from this evidence that plants need more water when it is hot than when it is cool. The inference that is made is based on the explicit information in the excerpt. An inference is the best conclusion that you can make based on the information you have.

Determining the main idea of a passage

The main idea of a passage is what the passage is mostly about. It is the main point of the passage. Sometimes the main idea is stated in a passage by the use of a topic sentence either at the beginning of the passage or elsewhere. Sometimes the main idea may be found in the title of the passage. Oftentimes the main idea is not stated in the passage; the reader needs to determine it from the information or details in the passage. The main idea will become more and more obvious to a reader as detail after detail supports it. Some information in the passage may not be supporting, but most ideas and details will support the main idea. The main idea is filled out by the supporting details in a passage.

Decide what the main idea of the following excerpt is, "There are many processes in making coins:"

> The United States Mint makes our money. The government chooses the designs. Artists make a clay model, and then they create a plaster model. A steel mold is made from this plaster model. A metal alloy is used for the coins. One machine punches out the coin and another imprints it with the design.

The information in the excerpt deals with the processes of making coins. It details what happens first, second, third, and so on when making a coin. The main idea is not stated in the excerpt, so the reader needs to put the details together to determine what it is. All of the details support the main idea being, "There are many process in making coins." All of the details describe these processes. The details about how coins are made are explicit: they are facts that can be checked. The central idea emerges from these facts and is shaped by the details that tell about the coin making processes. This is what supporting details do. They shape or tell more about the main idea so that the reader can tell what a passage is mostly about.

Objective summary

An objective summary of an informational text tells what the main idea of the text is and includes the important details. It tells what the text is mostly about and includes the most important supporting details. A summary should not include too much information; it is not a paraphrase of the information. It is important to select only the most important details to include. A summary should also be objective. This is achieved by focusing on the main idea rather than any opinions that might be in the text but that are not related to the main idea. It would also not include any personal opinions on the subject.

Read the summary and explain how to improve it:

> Edgar Degas was a great artist who broke with tradition and became an Impressionist. His paintings and sculptures are included in the collections of major museums everywhere. In his forties, his vision became poor and he worked more on sculptures because he could feel them. He died in 1917 at the age of 83. His father was a banker.

This summary is quite good. It has a main idea and includes some of the important details. The main idea is that Degas was a great artist. Supporting details include that his paintings and sculpture are included in collections of major museums as well as the fact that he had poor vision and turned to sculpting because he could feel the sculptures. While the information about his death is not perhaps the most important, it is of interest that he lived to the age of 83. The one glaring error with the summary is that it mentions the fact that his father was a banker. This does not directly relate to the main idea. It is not a supporting detail and is unimportant to the central thesis of the passage. It should be deleted.

Techniques used by authors

There are various techniques that authors use to make connections among and distinctions between individuals, ideas, or events. An author may choose to compare and contrast individuals, ideas, or events. This allows the reader to quickly see how something or someone is similar to or different from another thing or person. A second technique is through the use of analogies. An author may liken an idea, individual, or events by using analogies to show how they are similar and make her point clearer. An author might also put individuals, ideas, or events into categories to show how they are linked.

Read the excerpt and tell how the author makes connections between ideas:

> On the exterior it looked tidy and pleasant—a little log cabin with a fence around it. The lawn was cut close and the bushes were all tended to. No weeds in this yard. Inside was another story. The furniture was covered with dust. Huge spider webs dangled from the ceiling, and the floor was covered with dirt.

The author is comparing and contrasting the outside of a cabin with the inside. This is how the ideas are connected. Although the exterior looked tidy and pleasant, the interior was completely the opposite. It was dusty and dirty and had not been cleaned in a long time. Writers often link ideas. When a compare-and-contrast connection is made, the reader is quick to see the similarities and the differences between the two ideas or people being compared. Other ways to connect ideas is through categorizing. This technique is often used in scientific texts. Analogy is another way to connect ideas. This shows the relationship between two things or people so it is clearer to a reader.

Context clues

Context clues are an important resource when it comes to understanding the meaning of unknown words and phrases. Hints to the meaning of a word or phrase may be found in either the sentence in which the word or phrase is used or the sentences immediately before and after it. When determined the meaning of the word or phrase, substitute the synonym that you have for the unknown word or phrase. If it is still understandable, it is likely you have determining the meaning of the word. Figurative usage can also often be determined from the context of the text. Sometimes when reading technical text, it may be necessary to read more of the document to determine the meaning of a word.

Determine the meaning of "cordial" in the following excerpt:

> The salesperson smiled when the couple came into the store. She told them to take their time in choosing a ring. She chatted with them about their future plans. She was the most cordial salesperson they had ever met.

The excerpt states that the salesperson smiled. It says that she told them to take their time and that she chatted with them. Obviously the word "cordial" has a positive meaning based on these context clues. They seem to like the salesperson. She seems very pleasant. If you put the word "pleasant" in place of "cordial," the sentences make sense. Through this process it is possible to use context clues to help the reader understand the meaning of an unknown word. The same process can be used to decipher the meanings of unknown expressions or sayings.

Determine the meaning of "sense of foreboding:"

> All day long Ron kept thinking about Sue. For some unknown reason he was worried about her. He had a strong sense of foreboding that something was about to go wrong in Sue's city. His fear was well-founded. Early the next morning, there was an earthquake. But fortunately, it was mild. Sue was shaken but unharmed.

The passage says that Ron kept thinking about Sue and that he was worried about her. Then it says that his fear was well-founded because there was an earthquake. From this the reader can determine what a "sense of foreboding" means. It means having a feeling that something bad will happen. If you substitute that phrase for "sense of foreboding," it makes sense. This process helps you understand what a word or phrase means. Always check for clues in the sentence and surrounding sentences to determine the meaning of unknown words or phrases.

Read the excerpt and determine the meaning of "contusion:"

> Eli had fallen off the swing and his mother was very upset when she saw the swelling on his forehead. She rushed him to the emergency room. Dr. Vargas examined Eli and told his mother that it was just a contusion and nothing to worry about.

In this passage, the word "contusion" is a technical term. The reader can tell that it is a medical term because the doctor tells Eli's mother that is what he has. By reading through the passage, the reader will notice certain context clues that will help to determine the meaning of the word. Eli's mother saw a swelling on the child's head and took him to the emergency room. After the doctor examined the boy, she said the mother had nothing to worry about. The word "swelling" is key here. It suggests that "contusion" means a bump. If you replace "contusion" with "bump," the passage makes sense.

Figurative language

Figurative language is the use of ordinary words in a non-literal way or non-traditional manner. Figurative language is used by writers to expand their vision by creating images to make their writing more vivid and fresh. The literal meaning of a word or phrase is changed from its literal meaning to a figurative one. There are many different kinds of figurative language. A *simile* compares two things using the words "as" or "like." For example, "She was as clever as a fox." A *metaphor* compares two things without using the comparing words: "He was a fox when it came to getting out of a bad situation." *Personification* gives a thing or animal human traits. For example, "The fox cried out to him." When reading, look for non-traditional ways of using language that will contain hints to the meaning of the passage.

Which figurative language is used in the excerpt?

> We stood on the edge of the beach, a browned desert that offered no safe refuge, and watched the faltering ship struggling in the sea.

This is an example of a metaphor. The beach is likened to a browned desert that offered no safe refuge. They are compared without the use of the comparison words "as" or "like," so it is not a simile. The metaphor paints the beach in a negative way because it is compared to a desert with no safe refuge. The image adds vividness to the writing that would not exist if this image had not been added; it tells the reader what the author thinks of what is happening. It also suggests that something terrible is happening to the ship.

Denotative vs. connotative meaning of words

The *denotative meaning* of a word is the meaning that is found in a dictionary. It is the literal definition of a word. The connotative meaning is somewhat more subtle; it may also be listed in a dictionary, but after the literal meaning. The *connotative meaning* is what is suggested by or hinted at by a word, but not stated outright. The connotative meaning comes from the usage of the word. Its hidden meaning has come from personal experience. For instance, the words "lovely" and "exquisite" both mean "attractive," but "exquisite" suggests someone who is gorgeous or perfect-looking while "lovely" is less strong. When reading texts, you should always pay attention to words that have strong connotations because these words are a key to the author's opinion or point of view.

Read the following and explain the connotative meaning of the word "chef" and how it compares to "cook:"

> I have always thought of myself as a chef, not a cook.

Both the words "chef" and "cook" can be defined as "someone who prepares food," but the word "chef" carries a higher status than "cook." It suggests someone who prepares food professionally rather than someone who merely prepares food as a necessity, such as for a family. The speaker obviously thinks highly of her cooking ability and prefers to think of herself as a professional. When you are reading, pay close attention to what a writer is suggesting through the choice of word. When you are writing, choose words carefully so that you don't depict something in a negative way by mistake. Utilize a dictionary and thesaurus to help you find the perfect word.

Analogy vs. allusion

An *analogy* is a relationship; it can be a relationship between two things, people, or even words. When reading a text, look for words that signify an analogy, such as "like" or "the same as." A writer might say that his situation is about the same as being stranded on a desert island. That becomes an image for what he feels. It helps make his frame of mind clearer. In the same way, an *allusion* will make a point clearer. Writers often allude to another circumstance or event to clarify their own experience. For instance, in the following sentence, the allusion to a fairy tale tells you what the writer is trying to say: "I'm working harder than Cinderella, but I don't see a prince in my future." The allusion to the famous fairy tale tells you that the speaker is not very happy.

Analyzing the structure of a paragraph

When reading a paragraph, a close study of the way in which is it structured is helpful. The reader should first look to see how the author begins the paragraph. Does she open the paragraph with a topic sentence or does she use some other technique, such as a humorous or dramatic statement, to begin the paragraph? If the second is true, does a topic sentence follow or do supporting details come next? If the topic sentence is at the start of the paragraph, supporting details would follow it. The last sentence is the conclusion. Some conclusions can be topic sentences, but that is not usual. The last sentence most often brings closure to the paragraph and signals the end. Paragraphs can also have an overall structure. The structures of a paragraph include: a comparison and contrast structure, a cause and effect structure, a sequential structure, or a problem and solution structure. The structure of the paragraph depends a great deal on its main idea.

Determine the structure of this paragraph:

> The starfish hunts for clams in a strange way. When a starfish finds a clam, it wraps some of its arms around the clam. Then it pulls the clam open. After this, the starfish opens its mouth and pushes its stomach out of its mouth. The stomach goes into the clam shell and eats the clam and the starfish swallows its stomach again.

The paragraph opens with a topic sentence: "The starfish hunts for clams in a strange way." This sentence tells what the paragraph will be about. The other sentences are supporting details. They tell more about the main idea. The last sentence tells what happens at the end of the process of a starfish eating a clam. It provides closure. In determining the overall structure, the reader can use an elimination process. There is nothing to compare to the clam, so it is not a compare-and-contrast structure. There is no cause and effect structure indicated, nor is there a problem-and-resolution structure. The overall structure is sequential. The paragraph tells what happens in the order that it occurs.

Determining an author's point of view

The author's point of view is not always immediately clear. It could be stated clearly in many texts, but oftentimes the author does not want the reader to know exactly how he feels so a reader needs to discover it by the choice of words that an author uses, the information he includes, and any other relevant factors. It is important to read a text closely to determine what an author thinks about an event, person, topic or issue. Always check for any emotional statements that will give an idea of what the author is feeling. Look for any judgments an author may make about his topic, and piece together what you believe is the author's point of view.

How an author should acknowledge and respond to conflicting evidence or viewpoints

When discussing a controversial subject, an author has a duty to bring up both sides of an argument. The author may feel a certain way, but should still include opposing viewpoints in order to have a seemingly objective passage or essay. An author can, of course, refute the viewpoints but would need to use logical reasons why and cite any evidence that she wishes to include as testimony. In some cases, the author may not wish to side with either position, but merely to address the issues and give conflicting evidence so that the reader can form his own opinion about an issue.

Determine the author's point of view in the excerpt:

> Although flawed in some aspects, the play certainly kept the audience's attention, and there were cheers at the end. I look forward to Clemente's next play.

Based on what the author says in the excerpt, it would appear that he liked Clemente's play, even though he acknowledges some problems with it. He says as much by saying that, in spite of being "flawed" in some ways, the audience seemed to like the play because "there were cheers at the end." Then he goes on to say that he looks forward to Clemente's next play, which is the major suggestion that he, just like the audience, enjoyed the performance. It is important to read a text closely to determine what the author's opinion is by what he says and suggests.

Determining the purpose of the text

While reading a text, you should always try to determine its purpose. To do so, ask yourself why the author wrote the text and what affect the writing has on you. Is the purpose to explain something or tell how to do something? Does the text try to persuade you of something? Perhaps the text is making an appeal to your emotions. The signs that a text is attempting to persuade you include an author offering an opinion and telling why she thinks that way. On the other hand, if a text is simply informative, it will have many facts that will give details about an event or person or a thing, but not try to persuade you of anything. Manuals that come with equipment are clearly not persuasive; they simply are instructive.

Describe the purpose of this excerpt:

> Bristlecone pines are remarkable. They are the longest-lived form of plant life in the world. These trees can live as long as 5,000 years. Some bristlecone pines standing today in the western United States were seedlings when the Egyptian pyramids were being built. They were mature trees by the year 1 AD.

The purpose of the excerpt is to inform. The way in which a reader can tell this is that the text has concrete facts and details about the bristlecone pines. It does not have any opinions, other than the obvious one, that "bristlecone pines are remarkable." The author of the excerpt is not trying to persuade the reader of anything other than that. And the details that she includes make the pines very remarkable. The formal language is to the point and the information is interesting. The writer wants people to learn about the bristlecone pines; she is not selling them nor is she asking people to protect them.

Advantages and disadvantages of using different media

There are advantages and disadvantages to using different media. Print and digital texts are portable so you can bring them with you wherever you go. That is a distinct advantage, but the disadvantages are many in comparison with video or multimedia. For instance, if you are interested in learning how to cook a certain dish, you can read a recipe, but seeing a video would be much more informative. If you are reading an autobiography of someone, then a multimedia presentation will allow you to hear recordings of a person or see an actor playing the person, and that may bring the book to life. This is the primary difference between print and performed versions.

How a movie version of Superman would be different from a comic book version

A movie version of Superman would be quite different from a comic book version because an actor would play the superhero and would speak as well as actually fly through the air. The comic book version would mean that the person would only be able to read the dialogue, not hear it. The pictures in the comic book would show what Superman is doing, but there would be no movement in the images as there would be in a movie. The movie could have special effects and special lighting to make the plot scarier or tenser, but such techniques are likely not as effective in a comic book version.

Practice Test

Practice Questions

Read the following passage from Robert Frost's poem "The Road Not Taken" to answer questions 1-5:

Two roads diverged in a yellow wood,
And sorry I could not travel both
And be one traveler, long I stood
And looked down one as far as I could
5   To where it bent in the undergrowth;
Then took the other, as just as fair,
And having perhaps the better claim,
Because it was grassy and wanted wear;
Though as for that the passing there
10   Had worn them really about the same,
And both that morning equally lay
In leaves no step had trodden black.
Oh, I kept the first for another day!
Yet knowing how way leads on to way,
15   I doubted if I should ever come back.
I shall be telling this with a sigh
Somewhere ages and ages hence:
Two roads diverged in a wood, and I—
I took the one less travelled by,
20   And that has made all the difference.

1. What can be said about the author's tone in "The Road Not Taken"?

Ⓐ He feels some remorse about his decision.

Ⓑ He feels that he has accomplished something great.

Ⓒ He feels that his path has been different.

Ⓓ He feels that he should not have gone into the woods.

2. How does the point of view affect the tone of this poem?

Ⓐ It creates a feeling of superiority in the reader.

Ⓑ It causes the reader to feel slightly distanced from the scene.

Ⓒ It makes the reader feel as if he/she is making the same decision.

Ⓓ It causes the reader to feel as if he/she has no choice.

3. What is the main theme in this poem?

Ⓐ Deciding which road to take while on a hike

Ⓑ Making choices that may be different from others

Ⓒ How to make the best of a decision in the past

Ⓓ Wondering about the choices that others have made

4. What is the setting of this poem?

Ⓐ The early morning, near some wood in the early or late spring

Ⓑ The edges of a well-worn path near thick undergrowth

Ⓒ Two paths that are near a more traveled one in the late morning

Ⓓ The morning, in an autumnal forest with two walking paths ✓

5. Which lines from this poem show a kind of irony?

Ⓐ 16, 17, and 20

Ⓑ 4, 5 and 6

Ⓒ 6 and 8

Ⓓ 18 and 19

Read the following passage from Heywood Broun's The Fifty-First Dragon *to answer questions 6-10:*

> OF all the pupils at the knight school Gawaine le Cœur-Hardy was among the least promising. He was tall and sturdy, but his instructors soon discovered that he lacked spirit. He would hide in the woods when the jousting class was called, although his companions and members of the faculty sought to appeal to his better nature by shouting to him to come out and break his neck like a man. Even when they told him that the lances were padded, the horses no more than ponies and the field unusually soft for late autumn, Gawaine refused to grow enthusiastic. The Headmaster and the Assistant Professor of Pleasaunce were discussing the case one spring afternoon and the Assistant Professor could see no remedy but expulsion.
>
> "No," said the Headmaster, as he looked out at the purple hills which ringed the school, "I think I'll train him to slay dragons."
>
> "He might be killed," objected the Assistant Professor.
>
> "So he might," replied the Headmaster brightly, but he added, more soberly, "we must consider the greater good. We are responsible for the formation of this lad's character."

"Are the dragons particularly bad this year?" interrupted the Assistant Professor. This was characteristic. He always seemed restive when the head of the school began to talk ethics and the ideals of the institution.

"I've never known them worse," replied the Headmaster. "Up in the hills to the south last week they killed a number of peasants, two cows and a prize pig. And if this dry spell holds there's no telling when they may start a forest fire simply by breathing around indiscriminately."

"Would any refund on the tuition fee be necessary in case of an accident to young Cœur-Hardy?"

"No," the principal answered, judicially, "that's all covered in the contract. But as a matter of fact he won't be killed. Before I send him up in the hills I'm going to give him a magic word."

"That's a good idea," said the Professor. "Sometimes they work wonders."

6. What is the best way to describe Gawaine's character?

Ⓐ Fearless and excitable

Ⓑ Careless and frigid

Ⓒ Spiritual and careful

Ⓓ Cowardly and apathetic

7. What is the meaning of "his better nature"?

Ⓐ An increased sense of honesty

Ⓑ A man's ignoble ideas

Ⓒ A desire for propriety

Ⓓ A man's nobler instincts

8. How does the Headmaster put the professor at ease about Gawaine?

Ⓐ He tells him that Gawaine will only fight small dragons.

Ⓑ He assures him that Gawaine's contract has not expired.

Ⓒ He talks to him about the animals that have been killed by the dragons.

Ⓓ He mentions that Gawaine will be given a magic word.

9. What would be a good question for the Headmaster to consider?

Ⓐ Will Gawaine try hard to fight the dragons?

🅑 Will Gawaine want to learn about fighting dragons?

Ⓒ Will the professor let Gawaine learn about dragons?

Ⓓ Will the professor teach Gawaine to fight the dragons?

10. Suppose that Gawaine's parents have him removed from the school. Would the Headmaster still want Gawaine to learn to fight dragons?

Ⓐ No, he would be happy with the tuition payment.

Ⓑ No, he would think that Gawaine would eventually return.

Ⓒ Yes, because Gawaine is naturally very tall and strong.

🅓 Yes, because Gawaine will get a special word for protection.

Questions 11 -22 pertain to the following passage:
Call of the Wild by Jack London

(1) Buck did not read the newspapers, or he would have known that trouble was brewing, not alone for himself, but for every tide-water dog, strong of muscle and with warm, long hair, from Puget Sound to San Diego. Because men, groping in the Arctic darkness, had found a yellow metal, and because steamship and transportation companies were booming the find, thousands of men were rushing into the Northland. These men wanted dogs, and the dogs they wanted were heavy dogs, with strong muscles by which to toil, and furry coats to protect them from the frost.

(2) Buck lived at a big house in the sun-kissed Santa Clara Valley. Judge Miller's place, it was called. It stood back from the road, half hidden among the trees, through which glimpses could be caught of the wide cool veranda that ran around its four sides. The house was approached by gravelled driveways which wound about through wide-spreading lawns and under the interlacing boughs of tall poplars. At the rear things were on even a more spacious scale than at the front. There were great stables, where a dozen grooms and boys held forth, rows of vine-clad servants' cottages, an endless and orderly array of outhouses, long grape arbors, green pastures, orchards, and berry patches. Then there was the pumping plant for the artesian well, and the big cement tank where Judge Miller's boys took their morning plunge and kept cool in the hot afternoon.

(3) And over this great demesne Buck ruled. Here he was born, and here he had lived the four years of his life. It was true, there were other dogs, There could not but be other dogs on so vast a place, but they did not count. They came and went, resided in the populous kennels, or lived obscurely in the recesses of the house after the fashion of Toots, the Japanese pug, or Ysabel, the Mexican hairless,—strange creatures that rarely put nose out of doors or

set foot to ground. On the other hand, there were the fox terriers, a score of them at least, who yelped fearful promises at Toots and Ysabel looking out of the windows at them and protected by a legion of housemaids armed with brooms and mops.

(4) But Buck was neither house-dog nor kennel-dog. The whole realm was his. He plunged into the swimming tank or went hunting with the Judge's sons; he escorted Mollie and Alice, the Judge's daughters, on long twilight or early morning rambles; on wintry nights he lay at the Judge's feet before the roaring library fire; he carried the Judge's grandsons on his back, or rolled them in the grass, and guarded their footsteps through wild adventures down to the fountain in the stable yard, and even beyond, where the paddocks were, and the berry patches. Among the terriers he stalked imperiously, and Toots and Ysabel he utterly ignored, for he was king,—king over all creeping, crawling, flying things of Judge Miller's place, humans included.

(5) His father, Elmo, a huge St. Bernard, had been the Judge's inseparable companion, and Buck bid fair to follow in the way of his father. He was not so large,—he weighed only one hundred and forty pounds,—for his mother, Shep, had been a Scotch shepherd dog. Nevertheless, one hundred and forty pounds, to which was added the dignity that comes of good living and universal respect, enabled him to carry himself in right royal fashion. During the four years since his puppyhood he had lived the life of a sated aristocrat; he had a fine pride in himself, was even a trifle egotistical, as country gentlemen sometimes become because of their insular situation. But he had saved himself by not becoming a mere pampered house-dog. Hunting and kindred outdoor delights had kept down the fat and hardened his muscles; and to him, as to the cold-tubbing races, the love of water had been a tonic and a health preserver.

(6) And this was the manner of dog Buck was in the fall of 1897, when the Klondike strike dragged men from all the world into the frozen North. But Buck did not read the newspapers, and he did not know that Manuel, one of the gardener's helpers, was an undesirable acquaintance. Manuel had one besetting sin. He loved to play Chinese lottery. Also, in his gambling, he had one besetting weakness—faith in a system; and this made his damnation certain. For to play a system requires money, while the wages of a gardener's helper do not lap over the needs of a wife and numerous progeny.

(7) The Judge was at a meeting of the Raisin Growers' Association, and the boys were busy organizing an athletic club, on the memorable night of Manuel's treachery. No one saw him and Buck go off through the orchard on what Buck imagined was merely a stroll. And with the exception of a solitary man, no one saw them arrive at the little flag station known as College Park. This man talked with Manuel, and money chinked between them.

(8) "You might wrap up the goods before you deliver 'm," the stranger said gruffly, and Manuel doubled a piece of stout rope around Buck's neck under the collar.

11. What is the purpose of paragraphs 2-5?

Ⓐ To introduce all of the story's characters

Ⓑ To show Buck's personality

Ⓒ To introduce Buck

Ⓓ To show Buck's affection for Toots and Ysabel

12. Which sentence or phrase shows Buck's attitude about Judge Miller's place?

Ⓐ They came and went, resided in the populous kennels, or lived obscurely in the recesses of the house

Ⓑ The whole realm was his

Ⓒ He had a fine pride in himself

Ⓓ And to him, as to the cold-tubbing races, the love of water had been a tonic and a health preserver

13. The author uses the detail in paragraph 1 to

Ⓐ Describe Buck's life

Ⓑ Foreshadow Buck's story

Ⓒ Describe the story's setting

Ⓓ Introduce the story's villain

14. What is the significance of the Klondike strike in 1897?

Ⓐ It will lead to changes in Buck's life

Ⓑ It will cause more dogs to move to Judge Miller's place

Ⓒ It changed Elmo's life

Ⓓ It caused the Raisin Growers' Association to meet more frequently

15. The use of the word *imperiously* in paragraph four helps the reader know that Buck feels

Ⓐ Scared

Ⓑ Angry

Ⓒ Happy

Ⓓ Regal

16. The author organizes this selection mainly by

Ⓐ Describing Buck's life in the order in which it happened

Ⓑ Outlining Buck's history

● Showing Buck's life and then showing a moment of change

Ⓓ Comparing Buck's life at Judge Miller's place to what came afterwards

17. Which answer choice best describes the purpose of the selection?

● To set up a story by providing background information

Ⓑ To show Buck in a moment of heroism

Ⓒ To give details about the Klondike strike

Ⓓ To introduce all the dogs that live at Judge Miller's

18. In the future, Buck will probably

Ⓐ Continue to act like the king of Judge Miller's place

Ⓑ Reunite with his father, Elmo, and his mother, Shep

● Leave Judge Miller's place against his will

Ⓓ Spend more time in the garden

19. This selection is part of a longer work. Based on the selection, what might be a theme of the larger work?

● Change

Ⓑ Family

Ⓒ Hard work

Ⓓ Relationships

20. Paragraph 2 is mostly about:

Ⓐ The Santa Clara Valley

● Judge Miller's place

Ⓒ Buck's lifestyle

Ⓓ The Klondike strike

21. Which sentence from the passage foreshadows the rest of the story?

(A) And over this great demesne Buck ruled

(B) These men wanted dogs, and the dogs they wanted were heavy dogs, with strong muscles by which to toil, and furry coats to protect them from the frost

(C) His father, Elmo, a huge St. Bernard, had been the Judge's inseparable companion and Buck bid fair to follow in the way of his father

(D) But he had saved himself by not becoming a mere pampered house-dog

22. What's the most logical explanation why Buck doesn't read the newspapers?

(A) He's not interested in current events

(B) He's busy exploring Judge Miller's place

(C) The Raisin Growers' Association takes all his time

(D) He's a dog

Questions 23 – 26 pertain to the following passage:
Andy Grant's Pluck by Horatio Alger

(1) The house and everything about it seemed just as it did when he left at the beginning of the school term. But Andy looked at them with different eyes.

(2) Then he had been in good spirits, eager to return to his school work. Now something had happened, he did not yet know what.

(3) Mrs. Grant was in the back part of the house, and Andy was in the sitting room before she was fully aware of his presence. Then she came in from the kitchen, where she was preparing supper.

(4) Her face seemed careworn, but there was a smile upon it as she greeted her son.

(5) "Then you got my telegram?" she said. "I didn't think you would be here so soon."

(6) "I started at once, mother, for I felt anxious. What has happened? Are you all well?"

(7) "Yes, thank God, we are in fair health, but we have met with misfortune."

(8) "What is it?"

(9) "Nathan Lawrence, cashier of the bank in Benton, has disappeared with twenty thousand dollars of the bank's money."

(10) "What has that to do with father? He hasn't much money in that bank."

(11) "Your father is on Mr. Lawrence's bond to the amount of six thousand dollars."

(12) "I see," answered Andy, gravely, "How much will he lose?"

(13) "The whole of it."

(14) This, then, was what had happened. To a man in moderate circumstances, it must needs be a heavy blow.

(15) "I suppose it will make a great difference?" said Andy, inquiringly.

(16) "You can judge. Your father's property consists of this farm and three thousand dollars in government bonds. It will be necessary to sacrifice the bonds and place a mortgage of three thousand dollars on the farm."

(17) "How much is the farm worth?"

(18) "Not over six thousand dollars."

(19) "Then father's property is nearly all swept away."

(20) "Yes," said his mother, sadly. "Hereafter he will receive no help from outside interest, and will, besides, have to pay interest on a mortgage of three thousand dollars, at six per cent."

(21) "One hundred and eighty dollars."

(22) "Yes."

(23) "Altogether, then, it will diminish our income by rather more than three hundred dollars."

(24) "Yes, Andy."

(25) "That is about what my education has been costing father," said Andy, in a low voice.

(26) He began to see how this misfortune was going to affect him.

(27) "I am afraid," faltered Mrs. Grant, "that you will have to leave school."

(28) "Of course I must," said Andy, speaking with a cheerfulness which he did not feel. "And in place of going to college I must see how I can help father bear this burden."

(29) "It will be very hard upon you, Andy," said his mother, in a tone of sympathy.

(30) "I shall be sorry, of course, mother; but there are plenty of boys who don't go to college. I shall be no worse off than they."

(31) "I am glad you bear the disappointment so well, Andy. It is of you your father and I have thought chiefly since the blow fell upon us."

(32) "Who will advance father the money on mortgage, mother?"

(33) "Squire Carter has expressed a willingness to do so. He will be here this evening to talk it over."

(34) "I am sorry for that, mother. He is a hard man. If there is a chance to take advantage of father, he won't hesitate to do it."

23. **As it used in paragraph 1, the phrase *different eyes* means which of the following?**

Ⓐ Andy's eyes have changed color

Ⓑ Andy now wears glasses

⬤ Andy sees that the mood in the house has changed

Ⓓ Andy is happy to be home

24. Read this sentence from paragraph 14:

To a man in moderate circumstances, it must needs be a heavy blow.

The author uses the metaphor *a heavy blow* to indicate which of the following?

Ⓐ Andy's father is in a difficult situation

Ⓑ Andy won't be able to go back to school

Ⓒ Andy's father has lost over six thousand dollars

Ⓓ Andy is disappointed about his family's problems

25. Which of these is the best summary of the selection?

Ⓐ Andy Grant comes home from school and discovers that his father has won six thousand dollars. He will use the money to buy equipment for the farm. Andy finds out that he will need to leave school in order to help his father on the farm and work for Squire Carter

Ⓑ Andy Grant goes home and discovers that his family has fallen upon misfortune. Nathan Lawrence, the bank's cashier, has stolen twenty thousand dollars of Andy's father's money. Now that Andy's family has lost so much money, they won't be able to pay for his education and he'll have to leave school

Ⓒ Andy Grant's father has lost six thousand dollars because Nathan Lawrence stole it. This loss will cost Andy's family a lot of money. Since Andy's family pays $300 a month for his school, he will have to stop going to school. Andy is very cheerful that he doesn't have to go to school. He decides to work for Squire Carter in order to help his family

Ⓓ Andy Grant's family has suffered a misfortune because the bank's cashier stole money, some of which belonged to Andy's father. Without the money, Andy's family will have trouble paying its bills, including Andy's school bills. Andy will have to stop going to school. Furthermore, his father will have to borrow money

26. What phrase or sentence from the selection best shows Andy's feelings about having to leave school?

Ⓐ He began to see how this misfortune was going to affect him

Ⓑ Speaking with a cheerfulness which he did not feel

Ⓒ And in place of going to college I must see how I can help father bear this burden

Ⓓ I am sorry for that, mother

Questions 27 – 31 pertain to the following passage:
The Telegraph Boy by Horatio Alger

(1) Our hero found himself in a dirty apartment, provided with a bar, over which was a placard, inscribed:—

(2) "FREE LUNCH."

(3) "How much money have you got, Frank?" inquired Montagu Percy.

(4) "Twenty-five cents."

(5) "Lunch at this establishment is free," said Montagu; "but you are expected to order some drink. What will you have?"

(6) "I don't care for any drink except a glass of water."

(7) "All right; I will order for you, as the rules of the establishment require it; but I will drink your glass myself. Eat whatever you like."

(8) Frank took a sandwich from a plate on the counter and ate it with relish, for he was hungry. Meanwhile his companion emptied the two glasses, and ordered another.

(9) "Can you pay for these drinks?" asked the bar-tender, suspiciously.

(10) "Sir, I never order what I cannot pay for."

(11) "I don't know about that. You've been in here and taken lunch more than once without drinking anything."

(12) "It may be so. I will make up for it now. Another glass, please."

(13) "First pay for what you have already drunk."

(14) "Frank, hand me your money," said Montagu.

(15) Frank incautiously handed him his small stock of money, which he saw instantly transferred to the bar-tender.

(16) "That is right, I believe," said Montagu Percy.

(17) The bar-keeper nodded, and Percy, transferring his attention to the free lunch, stowed away a large amount.

(18) Frank observed with some uneasiness the transfer of his entire cash capital to the bar-tender; but concluded that Mr. Percy would refund a part after they went out. As they reached the street he broached the subject.

(19) "I didn't agree to pay for both dinners," he said, uneasily.

(20) "Of course not. It will be my treat next time. That will be fair, won't it?"

(21) "But I would rather you would give me back a part of my money. I may not see you again."

(22) "I will be in the Park to-morrow at one o'clock."

(23) "Give me back ten cents, then," said Frank, uneasily. "That was all the money I had."

(24) "I am really sorry, but I haven't a penny about me. I'll make it right to-morrow. Good-day, my young friend. Be virtuous and you will be happy."

(25) Frank looked after the shabby figure ruefully. He felt that he had been taken in and done for. His small capital had vanished, and he was adrift in the streets of a strange city without a penny.

27. Why did Frank give Mr. Percy all his money?

Ⓐ He was feeling generous

Ⓑ Mr. Percy offered to pay for the sandwiches

Ⓒ He owed it to Mr. Percy

Ⓓ He thought Mr. Percy would give him some of it back

28. What does the phrase "his small capital" mean in paragraph 25?

Ⓐ Frank's penny

Ⓑ Frank's twenty-five cents

Ⓒ Frank's virtuous nature

Ⓓ Frank's friendship with Mr. Percy

29. Why did Frank agree to eat lunch?

Ⓐ Mr. Percy was paying for it

Ⓑ Lunch was completely free

Ⓒ He only needed to buy a drink

Ⓓ He wanted to spend time with Mr. Percy

30. Is Mr. Percy likely to pay Frank back?

Ⓐ Yes, because he never orders what he cannot pay for

Ⓑ Yes, because he will be in the Park the next day at one o'clock

Ⓒ No, because Frank is not virtuous or happy

Ⓓ No, because he's shown that he does not have any money

31. What adjective best describes Frank's feelings in paragraph 25?

Ⓐ Disappointed

Ⓑ Incautious

Ⓒ Uneasy

Ⓓ Suspicious

Answers and Explanations

1. A: Line 16 reveals that the author will be talking about this moment later with a sigh. There is nothing in the poem to indicate that the author has done something great or that he should have not gone into the woods. While he does seem to say that his path has been different than others, that does not describe the tone of the poem.

2. C: The first person point of view makes the reader feel as if he/she is involved in making the same decision. The other choices involve other points of view: an omniscient reader would feel superior or even a little distanced from the scene. The reader also has a clear choice, so letter D would not be a good selection.

3. B: This is because the writer mentions there are two paths, and one seemed more worn than the other, showing it was more often used by travelers. The other choices involve reading too much into the poem.

4. D: The setting is laid out in lines 1 and 11.

5. A: Frost uses a type of irony called "verbal irony" here, and shows us his feelings by using expressions that go against what the literal words say.

6. D: Gawaine is said to be tall and sturdy, but would run away and hide at the smallest sign of trouble.

7. D: "His better nature" is a common way of talking about a person's deeper character.

8. D: Letter A is not mentioned in the text, and the other choices do not directly answer the question.

9. B: Considering Gawaine's character, this is the only choice that makes sense because it is well known that Gawaine is cowardly and the professor doesn't seem to know much about dragons.

10. A: This can be inferred from the text:
"Would any refund on the tuition fee be necessary in case of an accident to young Cœur-Hardy?"
"No," the principal answered, judicially, "that's all covered in the contract."

11. C: The correct answer choice is C because paragraphs 2-5 introduce Buck and the setting in which he lives. The paragraphs accomplish this introduction by giving many detailed facts, such as the detail in paragraph 5 about the times he escorted Mollie and Alice on walks. Choice A is incorrect because two new characters, Manuel and the stranger, are introduced in paragraphs 7 and 8. While aspects of paragraphs 2-5 show Buck's personality, choice B is incorrect because the paragraphs also give other details about Buck, such as information about his parents and appearance. Choice D is incorrect because Toots and Ysabel are only mentioned in paragraphs 3 and 4. Furthermore, paragraph 4 says that he utterly ignored Toots and Ysabel, not that he is affectionate towards them.

12. B: The correct answer is choice B because the sentence indicates that Buck felt as if he owned or ruled over Judge Miller's place. The word *realm* indicates that the sentence is

- 28 -

referring to everything. Choice A is incorrect because it talks about other dogs that came and went but does not show Buck's attitude towards them or Judge Miller's place. Choice C is incorrect because it shows Buck's opinion of himself but not his opinion of Judge Miller's place. Choice D is incorrect because it describes something that Buck enjoys, but does not give his attitude about the house and grounds at Judge Miller's.

13. B: The correct answer is choice B because details in the passage foreshadow what might happen to Buck. Phrases like "trouble was brewing" or "these men wanted dogs" indicate that one of the dogs men want or Buck might be heading for trouble. Choice A is incorrect because the paragraph does not give details about Buck's life; later paragraphs give those details. Choice C is incorrect because the paragraph does not give setting details. Setting details about Buck's current situation are given in later paragraphs. Choice D is incorrect because the paragraph does not describe any characters other than Buck; it does not indicate that Buck is the villain.

14. A: Choice A is the correct answer because the Klondike strike has caused people to look for dogs like Buck. Although paragraph 1 does not directly mention the Klondike strike, the reader can infer from paragraph 6 that the events discussed refer to the Klondike strike. Choice B is incorrect because paragraph 3 makes it clear that dogs came and went even before the Klondike strike. Choice C is incorrect because Elmo is Buck's father but not a main character in the story. Choice D is incorrect because the passage does not draw a connection between the Klondike strike and the frequency of the Raisin Growers' Association's meetings.

15. D: Choice D is correct because the sentence indicates that Buck considers himself to be like a king. Kings or royalty are often considered regal. Choice A is incorrect because nothing in the paragraph indicates that Buck is scared; in fact, Buck is like a king, which makes him unlikely to be scared of the other dogs. Choice B is incorrect because Buck doesn't indicate anger, which could be shown by barking or growling. Choice C is incorrect because *regal* is referring to Buck feeling like a king, which is unrelated to his happiness.

16. C: Choice C is correct because the first part of the passage mostly describes Buck's life, but the passage ends in a moment of change when the stranger wraps a piece of rope around Buck's neck. Choice A is incorrect because the passage does not describe a sequence of events as they happen. Instead the passage gives an overview of how Buck lived before the moment of change. Although part of the passage describes Buck's history, the passage also describes the moment in which his life changes, making choice B incorrect. Choice D is incorrect because the passage only describes life at Judge Miller's place but doesn't describe what came afterwards.

17. A: The correct answer is choice A because most of the passage provides background information about Buck's life and personality. Choice B is incorrect because the passage does not describe any moments in which Buck is acting heroic; instead, it describes Buck's regular interactions with the other people and animals at Judge Miller's place. Choice C is incorrect because the passage only briefly mentions the Klondike strike. The majority of the passage describes Buck's life. Choice D is incorrect because the other dogs are described in paragraphs 3 and 4. The rest of the passage focuses on Buck.

18. C: The correct answer is choice C because the stranger ties a rope around Buck's neck. This action indicates that Buck will be forced to leave Judge Miller's place. Choice A is incorrect because the end of the passage indicates that Buck might be forced to leave Judge Miller's place, which means he won't be able to continue to act like a king. Choice B is incorrect because the passage does not mention Buck or Shep at the end; Buck's parents are only mentioned in paragraph 5 when the passage describes Buck's family background. Although Manuel is a gardener, choice D is incorrect because Buck is likely leaving the garden to go away with the stranger, which means he won't be able to spend more time in the garden.

19. A: The best answer is choice A because the passage begins by setting up Buck's life and then showing a moment where his life is about to drastically change. Choice B is incorrect because only paragraph 5 refers to family; this is not a big enough portion of the passage to imply that the larger selection is about family. Although Buck might need to work hard in the future, choice C is incorrect because the passage does not have that many clues about upcoming hard work. Choice D is incorrect because the passage does not spend time showing that Buck strongly values relationships. The end of the passage indicates that Buck is about to experience a moment of change.

20. B: The best answer is choice B because paragraph 2 describes Judge Miller's place in great detail, including a description of the house, the driveway, the stables, and the outhouses. Choice A is incorrect because the paragraph only says that his place is in the Santa Clara Valley; however, the paragraph does not describe the valley in detail (it only describes it as sun-kissed). Choice C is incorrect because paragraphs 3 and 4 describe Buck's lifestyle, not paragraph 2. Choice D is incorrect because paragraph 2 does not mention the Klondike strike. The strike is referred to in paragraphs 1 and 6.

21. B: The correct answer is choice B because the sentence talks about how the men want dogs; the sentence foreshadows that Buck may be the type of dog that the men want. Choice A is incorrect because it refers to Buck's attitude around Judge Miller's place but does not hint at what might be coming next. Although part of the sentence indicates that Buck hopes to follow in Elmo's footsteps, the rest of the sentence simply describes Buck's father. Choice B better foreshadows what's going to happen in the story because it more closely relates to the events in paragraph 7 and 8. Choice D is incorrect because the sentence describes Buck's personality and interests without giving clues about what's going to happen next.

22. D: The best answer is choice D because, as a dog, Buck can't read. Although Buck may not be interested in current events, choice A is incorrect because choice D is a more logical answer. Choices B and C are also incorrect because the logic that Buck doesn't read the newspapers is drawn from the fact that dogs can't read.

23. C: The correct answer is C because Andy and his family were in good spirits, or happy, when he left for school at the beginning of the term. Now that he's returned, he knows something is wrong, but isn't sure what it is. Choice A is incorrect because the passage does not discuss Andy's eye color. The phrase *different eyes* is used metaphorically and does not literally mean that Andy has different eyes. For this reason, choice B is also incorrect. Choice D is incorrect because Andy is uneasy rather than happy. He knows something bad has happened.

24. A: Choice A is the correct answer because the phrase *a heavy blow* refers to the very difficult situation that Andy's father now finds himself in. The difficult situation hit him like a hammer, or heavy blow, because it was sudden and very financially painful. While it's true that Andy can't go back to school, choice B is incorrect because the sentence refers to Andy's father rather than Andy. Although losing six thousand dollars is part of the heavy blow, choice C is incorrect because the sentence does not show how much money Andy's father lost. The reader finds out the amount of money in paragraph 11, while the sentence in the question does not appear until paragraph 14. Choice D is incorrect because the sentence does not refer to Andy.

25. D: While parts of the other answer choices are correct, the best answer is choice D because it is the only choice that correctly summarizes the passage. Choice A is incorrect because Andy's father has not won six thousand dollars; he has lost that amount of money. Choice B is incorrect because Nathan Lawrence has stolen twenty thousand dollars, but only six thousand of that amount belonged to Andy's father. Choice C is incorrect because Andy is not cheerful that he doesn't have to go back to school; he likes school and is very disappointed.

26. B: The reader learns in paragraph 1 that Andy likes school. When Andy finds out he can't return to school, he is disappointed but he makes his voice sound cheerful when he's speaking to his family. Choice A is incorrect because it doesn't show Andy's feelings; it just shows that Andy knows how the family's misfortune will affect his studies. Choice C is incorrect because it simply contains Andy's new plans for the future and does not show his emotions. Choice D is incorrect even though this sentence does show Andy's emotions. However, this sentence refers to Andy's opinion about Squire Carter and not about returning to school.

27. D: Choice D is the correct answer. In paragraph 19, Frank says that he didn't agree to pay for both dinners, and then in paragraph 23 he asks for at least ten cents back. These two examples show that Frank thought Mr. Percy would return some of his money. Choice A is incorrect because Frank didn't intend to give all his money even though it may have been generous for Frank to buy Mr. Percy a drink. Choice B is incorrect because Mr. Percy didn't offer to pay for anything; in fact, he took money and didn't repay it. Choice C is incorrect because the passage does not indicate that Mr. Percy owes the money. Instead, it shows Mr. Percy tricking Frank in order to get Frank to buy him drinks.

28. B: The correct answer is choice B because the word *capital* refers to money. The reader can use the context of the passage to find the meaning of *capital*. Frank lost his twenty-five cents, which means his capital had vanished. Even though *capital* refers to money, choice A is incorrect because Frank had twenty-five cents rather than just a penny. Choice C is incorrect because Mr. Percy is the one who calls Frank virtuous. Choice D is incorrect because it's not clear if Frank had a friendship with Mr. Percy in the first place. Therefore, his friendship would not have vanished.

29. C: Frank knew he did not have much money, but when he saw that he would get a free lunch if he bought a drink, he was willing to eat it. Even though Mr. Percy handed the bartender the money, choice A is incorrect because Mr. Percy handed over Frank's money. Choice B is incorrect because lunch was not completely free; he needed to buy a drink in order to get the free sandwiches. Choice D is incorrect because nothing in the passage indicates that Frank wanted to spend time with Mr. Percy. Instead, paragraph 8 says that Frank was hungry.

30. D: Choice D is the best answer because Mr. Percy used Frank's money in order to get the drinks. Even though Mr. Percy claims that he'll pay Frank tomorrow, the reader can infer that he is probably lying. Choice C is incorrect because Mr. Percy tells Frank to be virtuous and happy as a way of dismissing Frank. However, he does not withhold the money because he feels that Frank is undeserving. Choice A is incorrect because Mr. Percy ordered drinks that he could not pay for with his own money. Although Mr. Percy says he'll be in the park, choice B is incorrect because Mr. Percy might be lying.

31. A: Choice A is the correct answer because Frank has realized that he has just lost all his money. The word *ruefully* shows that Frank is disappointed. Choice B is incorrect because Frank acted incautiously earlier in the passage when he gave Mr. Percy all his money. By paragraph 25, Frank is no longer incautious. Choice C is incorrect because Frank feels uneasy in paragraph 23. By paragraph 25, Frank realizes that Mr. Percy has cheated him. Choice D is incorrect because Frank is no longer suspicious about Mr. Percy's actions; he already knows that Mr. Percy is not going to repay him.

English

Function of an infinitive verb form

An *infinitive* is a verb form that is usually preceded by the word "to" and can be used as a noun, an adjective, or an adverb. When "to" is used before a verb, it is not a preposition but part of the infinitive form of the verb. An example of an infinitive used as a noun is: "To exercise is important." In this example, "to exercise" is the subject of the sentence. An example of an infinitive used as an adjective is: "She had the wisdom to travel."   The infinitive "to travel" modifies "wisdom." In the sentence, "We were happy to leave," the infinitive is an adverb that modifies the adjective "happy."

Moods of verbs

There are five moods that verbs can be formed in. The *indicative* is where a statement is made: "He leaves the house at 8 am." In the *interrogative*, a question is asked: "When does he leave the house?" The *imperative* is used for commands: "Leave the house at once!" In the *conditional*, a condition or wish is stated: "If he were smart, he would leave the house earlier." And in the *subjective*, a demand, recommendation, suggestion, or statement of necessity is made: "It is necessary that he be here on time." In the subjective and conditional forms, the verbs are distinctly different. For instance, in the example "If he were smart, he would leave the house earlier," the verb is a plural form rather than a singular form. In the sentence, "It is necessary that he be here on time" the correct verb form is "be" rather than "is."

Decide what error the following sentence has and how to correct it:

> To patch an inner tube, it is necessary that the cyclist is prepared.

This sentence is incorrect grammatically because the verb form is not the right one. The sentence is a recommendation and therefore requires a subjective verb form. The verb forms "am, "is" and "are" are replaced in a subjective sentence with the verb form "be." The corrected sentence would read: "To patch an inner tube, it is necessary that the cyclist be prepared." The choice of an incorrect verb form is very common. Subjective verb forms are used in formal language but not as much in colloquial English. The subjective voice is used for a sentence that indirectly expresses a demand, recommendation, suggestion or statement of necessity.

Read the following sentence and correct it:

> When the doctor turned on the instrument, a strange sound was heard.

This sentence is an example of an incorrect shift in the voice of the verb, something that is very common in colloquial English. The sentence starts out with an active verb, "turned on," and then shifts to a passive voice with "was heard." It can be corrected by rewording the second part of the sentence; the correct sentence reads: "When the doctor turned on the instrument, he heard a strange sound." Now both verb forms are in the active voice. The pronoun "he" agrees with its precedent "doctor." The active voice is preferred because it is stronger and more direct than the passive voice.

Read the following sentence and explain why and how it needs to be corrected:

Take a dose of medicine and then you should get some sleep.

This sentence shifts from an imperative verb mood to an indicative one. The verb moods in a sentence should match and these do not. There are two ways the sentence could be changed so the verb moods agree. Both verbs could be changed so they are in the imperative form. After doing this, the sentence would read: "Take a dose of medicine and get some sleep." You could also change both verbs to the indicative mood form: "You should take a dose of medicine and then you should get some sleep." Either sentence would be correct, although the second form is overly wordy. A shorter way of saying it would be: "You should take a dose of medicine and then get some sleep," where the second "you should" is understood.

Uses for the following punctuation marks: comma, ellipsis, and dash

Sometimes a comma, an ellipsis, and a dash are used to show that there should be a pause when text is read or spoken. A comma most often shows the need for a pause for before-and-after adverbs such as "therefore," "as a result," "however," "consequently" or before adverbs like "but," "while," and "so." A comma can be used after an introductory clause to show a pause as well. An ellipsis, or three small dots, can be used to show a pause in speaking when it is in the middle of a sentence that joins two ideas. A dash can also be used to show a pause when a parenthetical phrase is inserted into a sentence. However, the comma, ellipsis and dash are also used for other reasons, so do not assume that these are their only uses.

Correct the following sentence:

The news was however not as good as it might have been about the faltering ship.

There should be a comma before and after the word "however" to show that there is a pause. When reading a sentence like this, the voice naturally wants to pause around the word "however," which is the reason commas are placed around it. "However" is a conjunction and commas often set off conjunctions to allow for a pause. There are other reasons that commas are used as well. They are used to separate items on a list, for example. They are also used in the introduction and conclusion of a letter. The corrected sentence should read: "The news was, however, not as good as it might have been about the faltering ship."

Ellipsis

An ellipsis is used to show that a portion of a quote has been omitted. An ellipsis, which consists of three small dots, can come at the beginning, middle, or end of a quotation. The ellipsis should follow any existent punctuation in the quote. For example, the entire text of this quotation from John Donne is as follows: "No man is an island, entire of itself; every man is a piece of the continent, a part of the main." If you wished to omit a portion of the text, for instance the words "entire of itself," then you would punctuate it as, "No man is an island, … every man is a piece of the continent, a part of the main." When omitting something that comes after a period, put the period first and then three dots.

Correct the spelling errors in the following sentence:

> He put his foot on the accelerater and drove very quickely to the grandeose palace that the movie was using for it's setting.

The words that are misspelled are: "accelerater," which is spelled "accelerator"; "quickely," which is spelled "quickly"; "grandeose," which is spelled "grandiose"; and "it's," which should be "its." When writing, make sure to check in a dictionary to see how a word is spelled if you are unsure. Certain spelling rules will help, such as "I before E, except after C," (as in the word "receive") as well as "drop the final E" ("make" becomes "making,") and "double the last consonant" ("chop" becomes "chopping"). There are other skills that you can use to help you spell words correctly, such as sounding out words. By breaking longer words down into syllables, affixes and roots you may be able to determine the way a word is spelled. And in today's world, poor spellers are also assisted by software in word processing programs, such as spell check, which automatically lets you know if it suspects that a word is misspelled, although it is not 100 percent accurate.

Read the following sentence and change the verb to an active voice:

> The team was praised by the coach because of its record of wins.

To change the verb to an active voice the sentence should be rewritten as the following:

> The coach praised the team because of its record of wins.

The active voice is usually preferred because it is stronger. The passive voice can be used for effect, or might be used because no one knows who or what had caused an action. For instance, in the sentence, "The ball was broken," the reason the verb must be in the passive voice is that the reason the ball was broken is unknown. The passive voice is used when the writer does not want to emphasize the doer. It is frequently used in scientific texts.

Read the following sentence and analyze the verb:

> They spoke to her as if she were a child.

The verb form in the phrase "as if she were a child" is in the conditional form because it states a condition or a wish that is contrary to fact. Notice that this use of the conditional always requires the past tense. It also requires the plural form of the verb rather than the singular form. English speakers often make a mistake with the choice of verb. Although the conditional and subjunctive verb forms are not used a great deal in spoken English, they should be used when writing formal English.

Using context clues

Context clues are often found in the sentence that contains a new word or phrase as well as the sentences before and after it. A reader can often determine the meaning of an unknown word from these clues. For instance, a passage might say that the media have disseminated many foolish ideas about alligators. A reader might not be familiar with the word "disseminated," but then the passage goes on to say that some movies have implied that alligators spend their days waiting to attack an unsuspecting human being but, in fact, alligators usually feed on small animals like fish, snakes, and turtles, which live in or near the water and that it is very rare for an alligator to attack a human being. If you read this passage carefully, you can deduce that "disseminated" means "spread around." In this case, it means the spreading around of misinformation about alligators. Another helpful clue is that the word "disseminated" is in the position where a verb would go, so you would need another verb to take its place.

Use context clues to determine the meaning of "attribute" in the following excerpt:

> Some of the attributes of mammals are a backbone, warm blood, and the production of milk to nurse their young. In addition, almost all mammals bear living young. The platypus and the spiny anteater are exceptions. They lay eggs instead.

To determine the meaning of the word "attribute," the reader needs to analyze the rest of the sentence as well as the following sentences. It would appear that the excerpt is telling what mammals are like and what they have in common, with two exceptions. The excerpt says that mammals have a backbone, warm blood and that they produce milk to nurse their young. The word "attribute" as it is used is a noun, so you would look for another noun to replace it. If you substitute the words "trait" or "characteristic" for "attribute," the sentence seems to make sense. This is the way you can determine what a word or phrase means from the context clues that surround it.

Affixes and root words

A *root word* is a word before it is added onto. An *affix* is a prefix or suffix that is added onto a root word. Often, the affixes in the English language come from Latin or Greek origins. A *prefix* is added to the front of a root word and a *suffix* is added to the end of a root word. When you look at the meaning of a root word and the meaning of any affixes added to the root word, you can determine the approximate meaning of the word. For example, the root word "satisfied" means to be content with something. The prefix *dis-* means not. The reader can therefore determine that "dissatisfied" means to be not content with something.

Determine how the root and affixes of the word "precede" can help you determine its meaning:

You can determine the meaning of a word by studying its root and affixes. In the word "precede," the prefix *pre-* means "before." The root word "cede" comes from the Latin word "cedere," which means "to go." So the meaning of "precede" is fairly straightforward: it means "to go before." It is important for students to understand and study lists of prefixes and suffixes as well as root words and their meanings. This is a particularly good way to increase vocabulary and understand the origins of words. It is also useful when there is no context on which to determine the meaning of an unknown word.

Use general and specialized reference materials to find the pronunciation of a word

A print or digital dictionary can be used as a means to learn many things about a word. It will show the correct pronunciation of a word, tell its meaning, and its part of speech. The dictionary has a guide that shows how to sound out the words. It also lists all of the parts of speech that a word can be used as and the meanings it has in each form. In addition to the dictionary, the thesaurus is an extremely useful tool because it lists synonyms for all the various meanings a word can have, which helps you clarify the precise meaning as used in the context of the text you are reading. This means you can find other words to use in a report or text that mean the same as a word that may be used too often. Many books will have a glossary to help you with difficult or even technical words used in the text.

Anita was trying to verify the meaning of "brush" in the following sentence:

> She used her dictionary and found this.
> brush (brŭsh) *n.* 1. A device with bristles. 2. A light touch in passing. 3.
> Contact with something dangerous. *v. tr.* 4. To clean with a broom. 5. To
> touch lightly in passing.

Choose the correct definition of "brush" from the following sentence:

> Peter brushed by me to get to the buffet.

The correct answer is meaning 5: "to touch lightly in passing." If you substitute that definition for the word, the sentence makes sense. Meanings 1, 2, and 3 are nouns and do not fit with the context of the sentence. Meanings 4 and 5 are verbs and "brush" is used here as a verb, so it would have to be one of these definitions. When considering which meaning is being used, always check for context clues in the sentence or in the sentences before or after the sentence in which the word is used. Dictionaries also tell you how to pronounce words and what part of speech they are.

Verbal irony and puns

Verbal irony is a figure of speech in which the intended meaning of a statement actually is different, and usually the opposite, of what is said. It is often sarcastic in nature, as in the retort of the mother whose child is playing with her food and says, "Do I have to eat this food?" The mother simply says, "No, of course you don't have to eat it. Just eat it tomorrow when you are really hungry." The mother does not mean what she says in reality, but she makes the point that the food will still be there for tomorrow. A *pun* is a play on words: "He said that he would like to axe me a question, but he didn't think it would be knife to butt in on me."

Relationships between words

The relationships between words can often enlighten a reader as to their meaning. For instance, you may come across the word "colossal" and not understand what it means, but then you are told that it means the opposite of "little," giving you a good clue to its meaning. The same is true of synonyms. If someone said a synonym for "minuscule" is "tiny," you would understand the meaning of the word at once. Analogies can also be useful for understanding the meaning of words. If you are told that "foot" is to "toe" as "paw" is to "pad," then you get an idea of what a pad is from the analogy.

Distinguishing between the connotations and denotations of words

The *denotation* of a word is the dictionary definition of the word. The *connotation* of a word is what the word suggests beyond its dictionary meaning. It is both the meaning that people associate with that word and a subjective interpretation of the meaning of the word. The denotation meaning is objective. For instance, the words "bullheaded" and "resolute" mean "firm" or "persistent." But "bullheaded" carries a negative connotation because it suggests someone who is very stubborn. "Resolute," on the other hand, has better connotations because there is no suggestion that the term means "unreasonable." When you read, you should pay attention to the language that a writer uses to describe something. Look for words that suggest something about a place or person that are not directly stated in the text.

Determine what the connotations are of the words "audacious" and "brash."

The connotations of "audacious" and "brash" are different. While they both technically mean "bold," the word "brash" has a more negative connotation because it suggests someone who is hasty or even foolhardy. It could also suggest someone who is somewhat impolite. On the other hand, "audacious" has a slightly positive connotation because it means "daring" or "taking a chance" in a good way, possibly being brave. Writers often give their readers clues about characters, events, or places through the use of words that have strong connotations. It is important to study language used to describe things and people so such clues are not lost on the reader.

Improving comprehension

The acquisition of general academic and domain-specific words and phrases is especially important for success in academic endeavors. Without the ability to understand language at the high school level, a student will not be prepared for what he or she will encounter in the future, neither academically nor in life. Students must be familiar with domain-specific words and phrases if they hope to excel in a specific field. One excellent way to become proficient in language is to make lists of new words, use them in sentences, and learn to spell them. The glossary of a textbook is a good source for finding domain-specific words. Extended reading will allow the student to improve his or her vocabulary. Again, a good reader will try to understand the meaning of a word through context; should that fail, a student should find the precise meaning in a dictionary or glossary.

Practice Test

Practice Questions

Questions 1– 9 pertain to the following procedural essay:

How to Bake Beautiful Brownies

(1) Who doesn't love brownies. (2) For decades, this decadent dessert has been a favorite. (3) While some cooks still craft brownies from starch, there are many mixes available that produce perfect, chewy, chocolaty brownies. (4) In fact, with the help of a mix, you can bake beautiful brownies in three simple steps.

(5) The first step in baking beautiful brownies is preparing your tools and ingredients. (6) You will need a large mixing bowl, a sturdy mixing spoon, and a properly-sized baking pan. (7) You will also need cooking spray and, of course, the brownie mix and the ingredients listed on the package. (8) Spray the bottom of the baking pan with the cooking spray, and preheat the oven to 350 degrees Fahrenheit. (9) When you have assembled and prepared everything, your ready to start mixing.

(10) The second step in baking beautiful brownies is making the batter. (11) Next, add the oil, water, and eggs as directed on the package. (12) Dump the brownie mix into your mixing bowl. (13) Using the sturdy spoon, mix the batter approximately 50 strokes, or until everything is well-moistened. (14) When the batter is ready, pour it into the pan, smoothing the top with the back of the mixing spoon. (15) Finally, your brownies are ready to go into the oven.

(16) The last step in baking beautiful brownies is the actual baking. (17) Place the pan in the oven and set a timer for the appropriate time listed on the brownie mix packaging. (18) It is a good idea to check the brownies too or three minutes before the baking time is up to prevent over-baking. (19) When a toothpick inserted two inches from the edge of the pan comes out with moist crumbs on it the brownies are done. (20) Remove the brownies from the oven, and place them on a rack to cool.

(21) When the brownies are cool, cute them to the desired size. (22) Using a plastic knife to cut the brownies. (23) This will prevent tearing and create smooth cut lines. (24) Now, there's only one thing left to do—enjoy your beautifully-baked brownies. (25) You deserve them!

1. In sentence 1, what change, if any, needs to be made?

Ⓐ No change is needed.

Ⓑ Change the period to a question mark

Ⓒ Change the period to an exclamation point

Ⓓ Change the period to a comma

- 39 -

2. What change, if any, is necessary to improve the meaning and clarity of sentence 3?

Ⓐ No change is necessary.

Ⓑ Remove the comma after starch

Ⓒ Change craft to crave

Ⓓ Change starch to scratch

3. Which sentence functions as the thesis of this essay?

Ⓐ Sentence 2

Ⓑ Sentence 3

Ⓒ Sentence 4

Ⓓ Sentence 5

4. What is the problem with sentence 9?

Ⓐ Have should be had

Ⓑ Your should be you're

Ⓒ There should not be a comma after everything

Ⓓ Everything should be every thing

5. How could the sentence order be improved in the third paragraph?

Ⓐ Switch sentences 11 and 12

Ⓑ Switch sentences 13 and 14

Ⓒ Switch sentences 12 and 13

Ⓓ Switch sentences 14 and 15

6. What change, if any, is needed in sentence 18?

Ⓐ No change is needed.

Ⓑ Change too to two

Ⓒ Change three to 3

Ⓓ Insert a comma after up

7. What punctuation change is most appropriate in sentence 19?

   Ⓐ No change is needed.

   Ⓑ Insert a comma after out and a comma after it

   Ⓒ Insert a comma after it

   Ⓓ Replace the period with an exclamation point

8. What change, if any, is needed in sentence 21?

   Ⓐ No change is needed.

   Ⓑ Remove the comma after cool

   Ⓒ Change to to into

   Ⓓ Change cute to cut

9. How would you classify the problem with sentence 22?

   Ⓐ It is a gerund phrase, not a sentence

   Ⓑ It is an infinitive phrase, not a sentence

   Ⓒ It is a comma splice, not a sentence

   Ⓓ There is no error in sentence 22

Questions 10– 18 pertain to the following essay:

Road Trip

(1) Nothing says Summer like a family road trip. (2) There's just something about the sweaty, sweltering hours in a crowded car that makes each road trip seem like a memorable—if misguided—adventure. (3) I've been on several roadtrips in my life, and each one had its own special charm. (4) Above all other road trips, however, I will always remember my family trip to the Grand Canyon when I was twelve years old.

(5) The day we left was bright and cloudless. (6) I squeezed into the backseat between my little brother, Ronnie, and my big sister, Rebecca. (7) We piled the ingredients of a successful road trip around us, sodas, snacks, music, and games. (8) By the time we hit the freeway—a mere seven miles from our house—Ronnie and I had each already downed a whole soda and were starting on a second one, we were also halfway through a bag of chips. (9) What can I say? (10) We were growing boys. (11) Needless to say, we begged to stop at every rest area along the route, driving my father crazy. (12) Another thing that drove my father memorably crazy was our road games. (13) Twenty minutes into our drive, Rebecca began the alphabet game. (14) We started with the letter A, and each time one of us saw the next letter of the alphabet, we shouted it out. (15) There were long periods of silence as we watched road signs and license plates intently. (16) Then, when a letter appeared, we would all burst out shouting, and my startled father would swerve in surprise and yell at us to keep the noise down. (17)

The alphabet game was a source of grate amusement and a handful of fistfights during that never-ending trip.

(18) The trip wasn't all fun and games, however. (19) In fact, we had several disasters on our journey. (20) In retrospect, our challenges seem almost funny, but at the time, they seemed tragic. (21) We blue a tire on a lonely, dusty stretch of highway in triple-digit temperatures. (22) We caught some fish in a tiny, lakeside campground just across the Arizona border, but Mom turned our fish to charcoal over the campfire. (23) When we finally made it to the Grand Canyon, Rebecca fell on a rocky trail and broke her ankle. (24) We spent the rest of the trip in a dimly-lit hotel room, playing cards and watching movies so Rebecca wouldn't feel left out.

(25) Looking back, I'm sure it wasn't the trip my parents had planned for it to be. (26) But it was a trip I will never forget. (27) It was the imperfections that made the trip so memorable. (28) By the time we got home, we all hated each other a little and loved each other a lot.

10. What change, if any, needs to be made in sentence 1?

   Ⓐ No change is needed.

   Ⓑ Change says to say

   Ⓒ Change Summer to summer

   Ⓓ Change road trip to roadtrip

11. In sentence 3, what change is most appropriate?

   Ⓐ Change roadtrips to road trips

   Ⓑ Change been to being

   Ⓒ Change had to has

   Ⓓ Sentence 3 is correct as it is written.

12. Which sentence in paragraph 1 functions as the thesis of this essay?

   Ⓐ Sentence 1

   Ⓑ Sentence 2

   Ⓒ Sentence 3

   Ⓓ Sentence 4

- 42 -

13. How can the punctuation error in sentence 7 be corrected?

    Ⓐ Insert commas after ingredients and trip

    Ⓑ Change the comma after us to a colon

    Ⓒ Change the comma after us to a semicolon

    Ⓓ Remove the comma after music

14. What is the problem with sentence 8?

    Ⓐ There is no problem with sentence 8

    Ⓑ Sentence 8 is a sentence fragment

    Ⓒ Sentence 8 is a comma splice

    Ⓓ Sentence 8 has a misused infinitive phrase

15. In sentence 17, what change is most appropriate?

    Ⓐ Change grate to great

    Ⓑ Change handful to hand full

    Ⓒ Change fistfights to fist fights

    Ⓓ Change never-ending to never ending

16. What change, if any, should be made in sentence 21?

    Ⓐ No change is necessary.

    Ⓑ Change blue to blew

    Ⓒ Change highway to high-way

    Ⓓ Change triple-digit to triple digit

17. In sentence 23, which of the following is the most appropriate correction?

    Ⓐ Remove the comma after Canyon

    Ⓑ Insert a comma after trail

    Ⓒ Insert a comma after it

    Ⓓ Sentence 23 is correct as it is written

- 43 -

18. Which of the following sentences would make the best concluding sentence for this essay?

Ⓐ The alphabet game was the best part of all

Ⓑ In the end, it would have been more enjoyable if we had not blown a tire and Rebecca had not broken her ankle

Ⓒ The challenges we faced and the unexpected experiences made our Grand Canyon adventure the most memorable trip ever

Ⓓ I feel blessed to have such an adventurous family

Questions 19– 27 pertain to the following essay:

A Brief History of Basketball

(1) Basketball is, arguably, one of the most popular and most exciting sports of our time. (2) Behind this fast-paced sport, however, is a rich history. (3) There have been many changes made to the game over the years, but the essence remains the same. (4) From it's humble beginnings in 1891, basketball has grown to have worldwide appeal.

(5) One thing that sets the history of basketball apart from other major sports is the fact that it was created by just one man. (6) In 1891, Dr. James Naismith, a teacher and Presbyterian Minister, needed an indoor game to keep college students at the Springfield, Massachusetts YMCA Training School busy during long winter days. (7) This need prompted the creation of basketball, which was originally played by tossing a soccer ball into an empty peach basket nailed to the gym wall. (8) There was two teams, but only one basket in the original game.

(9) Dr. Naismith's YMCA game became so popular that teams began to form throughout the New England region. (10) Early games among these teams were rough and rowdy. (11) In fact, the games were generally played in steel or chicken-wire cages players often became injured when they crashed into these cages. (12) Over time, the metal cages were replaced by rope-mesh cages, reducing injuries and making basketball a more enjoyable game for the players.

(13) Just as the equipment for the game of basketball has changed over time the rules have changed as well. (14) The original game, as it was invented by Dr. Naismith, had only 13 rules written on two pages. (15) In contrast, the modern rulebook has more than 60 pages of rules! (16) Despite the increase in rules, the basics of basketball have not changed in more than a century, making it relatively simple to learn and play.

(17) Because of the simplicity of basketball, the game had spread across the nation within 30 years of its invention in Massachusetts. (18) As more teams formed, the need for a league became apparent. (19) The smaller National Basketball League (NBL) formed soon after. (20) On June 6, 1946, the Basketball Association of America (BAA) was formed. (21) In 1948, the BAA absconded the NBL, and the National Basketball Association (NBA) was born. (22) The NBA played its first full season in 1948-49 and is still going strong today.

(23) Though much has changed in our world since 1891, the popularity of the sport of basketball has remained strong. (24) From it's humble start in a

- 44 -

YMCA gym to the multi-million-dollar empire it is today, the simple fun of the sport has endured. (25) Although many changes have been made over the years, the essence of basketball has remained constant. (26) Its rich history and simplicity ensure that basketball will always be a popular sport around the world.

19. What correction, if any, needs to be made in sentence 1?

Ⓐ No correction is needed.

Ⓑ Remove the comma after arguably

Ⓒ Remove both commas

Ⓓ Insert a comma after popular

20. How would you correct sentence 4 in this essay?

Ⓐ Change beginnings to beginning

Ⓑ Change worldwide to world-wide

Ⓒ Change has to had

Ⓓ Change it's to its

21. What type of error is found in sentence 6?

Ⓐ Punctuation error

Ⓑ Wording error

Ⓒ Capitalization error

Ⓓ There is not an error in sentence 6

22. What correction, if any, is necessary in sentence 8?

Ⓐ No correction is necessary

Ⓑ Change was to were

Ⓒ Write the numbers as numerals instead of words

Ⓓ Remove the comma

23. What is the problem with sentence 11?

Ⓐ It is a run-on sentence

Ⓑ It is a comma splice

Ⓒ It is a sentence fragment

Ⓓ Sentence 11 is correct as it is written

24. What change, if any, is needed in sentence 13?

Ⓐ No change is needed

Ⓑ Insert a comma after equipment

Ⓒ Insert a comma after time

Ⓓ Insert a comma after changed

25. Which of the following changes would most improve the organization and clarity of paragraph 5 of this essay?

Ⓐ The paragraph is correct as it is written

Ⓑ Move sentence 18 to the beginning of the paragraph

Ⓒ Switch sentences 19 and 20

Ⓓ Switch sentences 21 and 22

26. Which of the following words would best replace the misused word absconded in sentence 21?

Ⓐ Appropriated

Ⓑ Ascended

Ⓒ Aborted

Ⓓ Absorbed

27. What change, if any, is needed in sentence 24?

Ⓐ No change is needed

Ⓑ Change it's to its

Ⓒ Remove the hyphens from multi-million-dollar

Ⓓ Remove the comma after today

Questions 28– 35 pertain to the following short story:

The Saga of "Sparky"

(1) Sparky was a loser, but he didn't stay that way. (2) You probably know Sparky better by his given name: Charles Schulz. (3) Nicknamed Sparky when he was a child, Charles schulz endured years of struggle before he finally found success. (4) Eventually, the loser became a winner. (5) Thanks to the hard work and perseverance of Sparky, the world will always remember a boy named Charlie Brown and the rest of the Peanuts gang.

(6) Sparky was born Charles Monroe Schulz on November 26, 1922, and he grew up in Minneapolis, Minnesota, where he struggled to fit in socially. (7)

He skipped two grades, and as a result he struggled with his studies. (8) He was also painfully shy, so he never dated. (9) In addition, Sparky was inert at most sports. (10) But he loved to draw, drawing was his dream.

(11) Sparky poured his heart and soul into his drawings during his high school years. (12) He had a particular love for cartooning, and he unsuccessfully submitted several cartoons to his yearbook. (13) In the late 1940s, when Sparky was in his mid-twenties, his dream began to come true. (14) Although he was devastated when the cartoons were rejected by the yearbook committee, he remained determined to make a living through his art someday. (15) He sold some cartoons to magazines and newspapers. (16) Someone finally appriciated his artistic ability.

(17) In 1950, Sparky created what would become his legacy; a comic called Peanuts. (18) The central character—Charlie Brown—was based on Sparky himself, and his lifelong struggle to fit in with the world around him. (19) Peanuts became an instant hit. (20) Adults and children alike were drawn to it because they could relate to the struggles of the characters.

(21) From its humble beginnings in the 1950s, Peanuts went on to become one of the most successful comics of all time. (22) Sparky lovingly hand-drew each of the 18,000 Peanuts comic strips, and they eventually appeared in over 2000 newspapers in more than 75 countries. (23) The Peanuts characters have appeared in comic strips, television specials, coloring books, children's books, and a variety of other media. (24) Although Sparky died in 2000, his work lives on. (25) His comics are still seen in dozens of newspapers each week. (26) Through hard work, perseverance, and believing in himself, Sparky turned his loser's lot into a story of success.

28. Which of the following is the most appropriate correction for sentence 3?

Ⓐ Change Sparky to sparky

Ⓑ Change Nicknamed to Nick-named

Ⓒ Remove the comma after child

Ⓓ Change Charles schulz to Charles Schulz

29. In sentence 9, what change is necessary?

Ⓐ Change inert to inept

Ⓑ Remove the comma after addition

Ⓒ Change Sparky to sparky

Ⓓ Change most to many

30. What change, if any, should be made in sentence 10?

Ⓐ No change is necessary

Ⓑ Remove the comma

Ⓒ Replace the comma with a semicolon

Ⓓ Replace the comma with a colon

31. What change would most improve the organization of the third paragraph of this composition?

Ⓐ Swap sentences 13 and 14

Ⓑ Move sentence 13 to the beginning of the paragraph

Ⓒ Swap sentences 11 and 16

Ⓓ Move sentence 12 to the end of the paragraph

32. What change, if any, should be made in sentence 16?

Ⓐ No change is necessary

Ⓑ Change finally to finaly

Ⓒ Change appriciated to appreciated

Ⓓ Change artistic to autistic

33. What change, if any, is needed in sentence 17?

Ⓐ No change is necessary

Ⓑ Replace the semicolon with a colon

Ⓒ Replace the semicolon with a period

Ⓓ Remove the semicolon

34. What punctuation change, if any, should be made in sentence 18?

Ⓐ No change is necessary

Ⓑ Remove the dashes

Ⓒ Replace the second dash with a comma

Ⓓ Replace the first dash with a colon

- 48 -

35. How does sentence 21 function as a transition between paragraph 4 and paragraph 5?

Ⓐ Sentence 21 does not function as a transition

Ⓑ It talks about a topic previously mentioned

Ⓒ It demonstrates transition with the phrase "went on"

Ⓓ It connects the history of Peanuts with the success of Sparky

Answers and Explanations

1. B: Sentence 1 is a question and needs a question mark as the end punctuation.

2. D: In this sentence, "scratch" is a better word choice than "starch." As written, that part of the sentence makes no sense, but it makes perfect sense if we replace "starch" with "scratch."

3. C: Sentence 4 functions as the thesis statement for this essay, clearly presenting the main idea of the entire piece, which is how to bake beautiful brownies. Generally, the thesis sentence of an article will have much in common with the article's title.

4. B: Changing "your" into "you're" is the appropriate correction for sentence 9. "Your" is a possessive pronoun, while "you're" is a contraction of "you are", which is what the author intended to say here.

5. A: Switching sentences 11 and 12 improves the order and clarity of the third paragraph by organizing the steps more chronologically. B, C, and D would actually further disrupt the chronological order of the paragraph.

6. B: The word "two" is the correct word for sentence 18, as the concept referenced is a number. The word "too" means also, besides, in addition to, etc.

7. A: Sentence 19 is correct as written; no change is needed.

8. D: The word "cute" is either a misspelling, or a typographical error; it should be "cut."

9. A: Sentence 22 is a sentence fragment consisting of nothing but a gerund phrase. It cannot stand alone as a sentence.

10. C: The word "summer" has been improperly capitalized in sentence 1. In ordinary usage, the names of the seasons should not be capitalized.

11. A: The phrase "road trip" should always be written as two words, not one. This holds true for the plural form of the phrase as well.

12. D: Sentence 4 functions as the thesis in this essay. It introduces the main point of the article, which is to describe the author's memorable road trip to the Grand Canyon as a child.

13. B: Changing the comma to a colon corrects the error in sentence 7 and prepares the reader for the list of items that follows.

14. C: Sentence 8 is a comma splice, which is a type of run-on sentence. A period should come after "one", and "we were also halfway through a bag of chips" should be converted into a complete sentence that stands alone.

15. A: The word "grate" is incorrect; it should be "great." Either the author made a spelling error, or he confused two words that sound exactly alike, but have two different meanings – "grate" and "great."

16. B: The word "blue"is a color. It should be replaced with the word "blew", which is a verb.

17. D: Sentence 19 is correct as written; no change is needed.

18. C: This is the best choice for a concluding sentence, because it's about the entire story. The other choices don't focus on the story as a whole, but only smaller parts of it.

19. A: Sentence 1 is correct as it is written.

20. D: The word "it's" in this sentence is used incorrectly, because it is a contraction of "it is", which makes no sense. The word should be "its", which is a possessive pronoun.

21. C: Sentence 6 contains a capitalization error. The word "minister" should not be capitalized unless it's part of a title. In this instance, it's not part of a title, but is used as a job description.

22. B: In the first clause of sentence 8, "teams" is plural, so it must have a plural verb to go with it. So "was" needs to be changed to "were."

23. A: Sentence 11 is a run-on sentence. It should be corrected by adding a semicolon after "cages."

24. C: Adding a comma after time separates the introductory clause from the main clause of the sentence.

25. C: Switching sentences 19 and 20 improves the organization and clarity of paragraph 5.

26. D: The word "absconded" means "went away secretly and in a hurry"; it makes no sense in this sentence. The word "absorbed" should replace it, to show that the two entities combined to form a single organization.

27. B: The word "its" in this sentence is used incorrectly, because it is actually a possessive pronoun. The word needed is "it's", which is a contraction of "it is."

28. D: Charles schulz should be changed to Charles Schulz.

29. A: Changing "inert" to "inept" corrects the meaning of sentence, because inert is not the correct word choice here. It means motionless, unable to move, barely moving, etc., while "inept" means unskilled. It's much more likely that the author meant to say that Charles Schulz was unskilled at sports, rather than saying that he just stood motionless while engaged in athletic endeavors.

30. C: Sentence 10 is a comma splice with two independent clauses, which is incorrect. Two independent clauses should be joined by a semicolon, not a comma.

31. A: Swapping sentences 13 and 14 will improve the organization and flow of paragraph 3, because they are out of chronological order as written. This is jarring and confusing to the reader.

32. C: The word "appreciated" is a misspelling; the correct spelling is "appreciated."

33. B: A colon is the correct punctuation in sentence 17, not a semicolon.

34. A: Sentence 18 is correct as written.

35. D: The author has been talking about Sparky's struggles to succeed, and the history of the Peanuts strip, and in the final paragraph he demonstrates just how successful Sparky became, all thanks to the popularity of Peanuts. Sentence 21 serves as a transitional sentence between these two aspects of the article.

Writing

Producing clear and coherent writing

Every type of writing has its own characteristics, but to attain clear and coherent writing, it is necessary to plan what you will be writing about. You need to decide what your goal is; are you trying to write a narrative or are you writing to inform or persuade? After you have decided on your goal, you need to organize your material, especially in the case of nonfiction writing. You need to have a clear picture of your main ideas and supporting details. If you are planning to write a narrative, you need to pay attention to both developing your story in a clear and flowing manner and to creating believable characters through use of precise language including descriptions, dialogue and action. Another requirement is the establishment of a tone that is appropriate to the task, purpose, and audience. Finally, make sure your writing is grammatically correct and has no spelling errors.

Constructive criticism

You can work with your peers and adults to improve your writing. Have them read what you are writing and suggest ways to change it. An important part of the process is planning what you want to write. After you complete a first draft, you will need to revise your text. Editing the text comes next and you must develop a critical eye to make sure that the grammar and verb usage are correct and that you are using an active voice rather than a passive one. Sometimes you will find your writing fails to achieve its purpose. If that happens, you may have to start over and try something different. You may want to introduce a chart to make the material easier to understand, or change the ending to a story you are writing. Lastly, you need to learn how to assess if you have addressed your purpose and audience. Ask yourself whether the writing accomplishes what you want it to and if the language is suitable for the audience you want to reach.

Decide why the following passage needs revision and how to revise it:

> Galileo was believing that the Earth moved around the Sun. They, the other teachers, did not believe that. He was sent to jail. Was being a brilliant mathematician. He was scorned by the other teachers at his university. They think him a foolish rebel. Now, we don't believe that he is considered a genius and a hero.

The writer of the passage has made a lot of grammatical mistakes. The style is not as formal as it should be and some sentences are almost incomprehensible. In the first sentence, an incorrect verb form is used. The second and fifth sentences seem to repeat the same information. The third sentence is not linked to the previous information. The fourth sentence does not have a subject. And the last sentence is a run-on. Here is one way to make those corrections:

Galileo believed that the Earth moved around the Sun. Because of this belief, he was sent to jail. Galileo was a brilliant mathematician. However, he was scorned by the other teachers at his university. In his own time, he was thought to be a foolish rebel. Now, he is considered a genius and a hero.

Now, the writing is much better organized and the mistakes are corrected.

Using the Internet

Online sources are invaluable tools. Writers can get works published at little or no cost as an e-book. There are other options available as well, such as editing and marketing services offered on many Internet sites. Some sites offer help with everything from style to grammar. Many sites can be used as credible research sources, where you find accurate and objective information for research projects and where you can compare information and ideas and how they may relate one to the other. Always cite all sources that you use from the Internet using the MLA (Modern Language Association) style as a guide. Additionally, the Internet has many sites where people can collaborate on projects. Chat rooms and topic websites are tools that allow an exchange of information as well as shared writing projects.

Conducting a short research project

When conducting a short research project to answer a question, draw up a list of keywords relating to the question. Use these words in a search engine to bring up websites that relate to the issue at hand. Use the most reliable websites for information to use in your research and be sure to keep track of the websites so that you can cite them in your text. While researching the subject, you will probably find related issues that would broaden the extent of your research project, so you may choose to come up with other keywords that would extend your research from its original scope. Make sure to draw from several sources when preparing your research paper. In that way, you can compare and contrast the information that is available.

When conducting research, your primary job is to list the kind of information you are looking for and then create a list of keywords to use for a search in multiple print and digital sources. Take extensive notes, noting the source that each bit of information comes from. Be sure to check on the reliability and credibility of each source. Journals, textbooks, magazines, and newspapers are all useful sources. Also, always verify how timely, accurate and credible your sources and information are. Dismiss any sources that seem questionable. When writing your report, you may paraphrase, but do not copy information down directly because that constitutes plagiarism. Use fresh language and attempt to rewrite the details and other information in your own language. Use the Modern Language Association (MLA) guidelines for all citations.

Analyze how the Bible is the basis of Andrew Lloyd Weber's musical Jesus Christ Superstar:

> Andrew Lloyd Weber's musical *Jesus Christ Superstar,* which dates from 1971, is loosely based on the last days of Christ's life from the Gospel and his relationship to Judas. However, many of the conversations and events included in the musical are not found in the Bible at all. *Jesus Christ Superstar* also makes use of songs and lyrics to bring the characters of Christ and Judas to life. It follows Christ's life from the time he and his disciples enter Jerusalem until the crucifixion, including Judas's betrayal of Christ. Judas is a very developed character in the musical and most of the action is the tension

- 54 -

between Christ and him. Weber, like many other modern artists, makes use of the story from the bible, but uses it in a modern way so that it is appealing to modern audiences. Some of the music from the musical is still popular today.

Terri is researching a paper on hurricanes. Evaluate the following sources as to their reliability:

> http://www.nhc.noaa.gov/
> http://en.wikipedia.org/wiki/
> Tropical_cyclone

When doing research on the Internet, you need to be extremely careful that the website you are using to get facts and details about a subject is authorized and credible. The first source is a highly credible one. It is the National Weather Service National Hurricane Center. The information on this site would be totally credible because it is run by a component of the National Centers for Environmental Prediction (NCEP) at the Florida International University in Miami, Florida. All the information that you find there is accurate and credible because it is run by scientists in that field. The second source is not so credible. Wikipedia is not considered a credible source. It is not supervised in the way that a professional encyclopedia is. There are many mistakes that are made in their information. No academic group would accept it as a reliable source.

Making writing a habit

It is important that students become habitual writers. The more a student writes, the more he will improve his writing. Whatever the purpose for writing, students should be able to formulate their ideas into words. Some tasks will be shorter than others and require less work. A letter to a friend may not be a long undertaking, but a report will require more effort and time, including rewriting and editing as well as proofreading the finished paper. But whether the writing assignment is short or long, students need to find a way to become communicators with the written word. This means employing proper grammar and spelling as well as varied syntax to keep the reader interested.

Persuasive Text

Introducing a claim

An excellent way to introduce a claim is to present evidence of its validity in a logical manner. The same can be true of distinguishing your claim from alternate or opposing claims. Logical evidence based on valid sources will give your claim strength. Central to organizing your reasons and evidence is doing excellent research and finding evidence that is based on facts and comes from experts in the field. Then the passage should be organized so that one idea flows from another and into the next. When writing, place your claim at the top and then list the reasons and evidence that support the statement. This will help you organize your passage logically.

When you present a claim, there should be supporting evidence that is reliable. Without credible evidence or sources, your argument will be weak. The evidence needs to be reliable and relevant and should cover every point that is made. It is vitally important that you do a great deal of research to develop your evidence. While researching, have a critical eye and anticipate what readers might say; this will help you to develop your claim thoroughly. It is not enough to research a claim on the Internet because many Internet sources are not reliable. When using the Internet, look for sites that are objective. Find experts that you can quote and use proven statistics. Make sure to present your information in a logical manner so that the reader can easily understand your argument.

Evaluating arguments and claims

When reading a persuasive essay, the reader will want to analyze and evaluate an argument and claims based on the validity of the evidence that is given. Claims are often made by authors, but it is important that these claims are backed with evidence. This evidence, however, must come from valid sources in order for it to be accepted. Sources include books that are written by experts on a subject, information from studies that are accredited, and Internet sources that are trustworthy. When analyzing a source, ask yourself if the source has any evidence of being an authority on the subject at hand.

Recognize irrelevant evidence

Claims are sometimes introduced but the evidence is not relevant to the subject of the text. It may be because the evidence does not come from a credible source, or because the evidence may have little to do with the claim. When evaluating evidence, ask yourself what relationship the evidence has to a claim. For instance, if a writer says that global warming is not occurring and then cites evidence from a study that is 25 years old, it is probably outdated and irrelevant to the claim. The reader should be aware of this possibility and disregard any irrelevant evidence. The reader should also be wary of any evidence that is not from a valid source.

Dealing with conflicting information

When confronted with information from two different texts that have conflicting information, the reader should decide whether the conflict is a matter of fact or interpretation. Often times, particularly in political texts, the same facts may be interpreted in different and conflicting ways. It is important for the reader to evaluate these facts and see if they are based on information that is credible. Then the reader must determine whether the various interpretations are supported by the facts. This is not always easy to do, but it is important for the reader to develop a critical eye for that very purpose.

Creating cohesion

The best way to create cohesion between claims, counterclaims and evidence is to organize your ideas and then write sentences explaining your reasons and evidence that follow your main ideas logically. Careful research will result in your argument being cohesive and easy to understand. Your claim and evidence must be clearly related to each other. Words that will indicate to the reader that the claim and evidence are related include "since," "because," "as a consequence" and "as a result." You can also utilize clauses to demonstrate a relationship between the reason and the effect. Consider the following sentence: "As a result of the following observations by scientist John Neal, more people have come to believe that a good night's sleep is necessary to being healthy." The sentence establishes causality between the reason and effect. When stating counterclaims, remember to use linking words such as "but" or "on the other hand" to indicate that an alternative claim will follow.

Maintaining a formal style

A formal style is used when writing essays, both persuasive and informative. This style helps the writer achieve objectivity and keep the language precise. Formal writing consists of complex words and sentences; sentence fragments should be avoided unless they are being used for a specific reason. The tone of the writing is serious. The third person is always used, not the first or second person. An active voice is preferred because it projects more energy than a passive voice. Contractions are not used in formal writing. Sentences should be grammatically correct, as should the spelling and punctuation. When writing, reread and edit your passage several times to improve it. Vary the kinds of sentences and make sure that your ideas follow a logical order as well.

Read the following passage and identify what style it is written in:

> About two hundred years ago, world literature was growing rapidly. At that time, publishing books became profitable because people had more free time and turned to reading for entertainment. It was, however, quite a different reading compared to previous periods when books were created only for the few and not the everyman.

The excerpt is written in a formal style. The first thing to notice is that the third person is used for the viewpoint. The piece also has a serious tone and uses precise language. The sentences are complex and varied and no contractions are used. All of these details point to a formal style. If it were an informal style, the first or second person would be used, the tone would be more casual, and the language would be more generalized than is evident in this excerpt.

Importance of have a concluding statement

A concluding statement is important for a persuasive passage because it follows from and supports the argument that has been stated earlier in the passage. It should sum up the main points of the passage and give the reader a sense of completion and the passage a sense of closure. The purpose of the concluding sentence is to pull all aspects of the passage together and make sense of the ideas, evidence and details that have been included previously. The concluding statement should also be memorable because it will be last chance the writer has to convince the reader of his or her argument.

What kind of argument would the following sentence best conclude?

> Physical activities help you become stronger, live longer, and make you happier.

The sentence would make a good concluding sentence for a passage about the reasons why one should adopt some form of physical activity. Arguments could include the benefits of different activities and why physical activity makes a person become stronger, live longer and be happier. The sentence was probably preceded with information on how to get started with a physical activity, such as being sure to check with a doctor before starting a new regimen, where a person can learn more about various forms of activities, and how to decide which activity is right for the reader. This sentence would provide closure for a passage of this type.

Informational or Explanatory Text

Introducing a topic

An informational or explanatory text should have an introduction to the topic that the text will feature. One way you can accomplish this is by using a topic sentence followed by details that support your thesis. Another tactic is to use a reference to a current event, even if your topic refers to something in history. Ideas should be organized in a logical manner, with supporting details coming after a main concept. Connections can be made between concepts by using connecting words such as "however," "since," and "as a result." Distinctions between ideas should also be made clear and can be signaled by words such as "but" or "on the other hand." Other organizational tips include choosing whether to include a specific relationship such as cause and effect, question and answer, or problem and solution.

Organizing ideas

There are many ways to present information so that it is easier to understand. One effective tool is headings. Each heading introduces a new concept or idea in a text and allows the reader to see, just by skimming, what the article is about and which points are being covered. Another useful tool is graphics. Graphics are extremely useful because they present a lot of detailed information in a visual form that is easy to understand. Instead of putting the information in a paragraph where it can be lost to the reader, it can be put into a graphic such as a chart or table that will make it much more approachable. Multimedia such as voice-over, videos or even movies are other excellent ways to present information; in this modern world, people respond very easily to this kind of presentation. Difficult material can be made much more enjoyable through the use of these tools.

Developing a topic

When developing a topic in an informational or explanatory text, it is vital that the text utilizes relevant facts that clearly support the main topic. After the introduction of the topic, claim or argument, concrete details and facts that are relevant should follow. The supporting details that are cited should be from reliable sources. At times, definitions of unfamiliar terms are appropriate. Quotations by experts in the field are also a good addition to a passage because they give credibility to the text and may make the subject more interesting to read about. The results of any research that might have been done would also be of interest. Examples or anecdotal incidents will also make a text more approachable.

Creating cohesion

The use of appropriate transition words helps to clarify the relationships between ideas and concepts and creates a more cohesive passage. A good writer knows that such words and phrases serve to indicate the relationship between ideas and concepts. Words or phrases that show causality between ideas include "as a result," "consequently" and "therefore."

Words that show a compare-and-contrast relationship include "however," "on the other hand," "in contrast" and "but." When introducing examples of different concepts, words such as "namely," "for example" and "for instance" act as transition words. Transition words such as "foremost," "primarily," "secondly," "former" and "latter" can be used when showing the order of importance of ideas or concepts.

Decide how the following sentences could be written so that there is a better transition between the ideas:

> It was time for the whales to breed. The whales were swimming south.

The author rewriting these two sentences should first understand their relationship to one another. There is a causality suggested here. The reason that the whales were swimming south is that it was time for them to breed. To combine the sentences, you need to use an appropriate transition word. In this case there are several options. The phrase "as a result" works well because it shows the causality between the two thoughts: "It was time for the whales to breed; as a result, the whales were swimming south." Other causality words such as "consequently" or "therefore" could also be used.

Importance of using precise language and domain-specific vocabulary

Writers of informational or explanatory texts need to use precise language and domain-specific vocabulary in order to express themselves clearly. General vocabulary words are not specific enough in many cases. A formal essay relies on the use of vocabulary that shows a mastery of a topic. Besides a main idea, details need to be included that are supplied by carefully chosen, precise and domain-specific language. Some of the terms will necessitate definitions, which can be included in the essay. While researching a subject, it is important to include technical vocabulary so that it can be used during the writing of the text.

Establish and maintain a formal style

Writers of informative or explanatory passages generally use a formal style because it has a greater sense of objectivity. The use of an informal style in informative or explanatory texts is not acceptable. A formal style always uses a third person. The formal style calls for complex and varied sentences. These will add a further tone of formality and depth to the subject. The use of a formal style shows the seriousness of a topic. Formal writing also includes clear and credible supporting details. Personal opinion rarely has a place in an informative or explanatory passage unless it can be justified in some way that is supported.

Rewrite the following so it is in a formal style:

> I've heard about volcanoes. I read that they are openings in the earth's surface. Lava, hot gases, and bits of rock come out of them. They are very forceful. I read that these volcanoes come from deep inside the earth.

Here is one way to re-write the passage:
Volcanoes are openings in the earth's surface from which lava, hot gases, and bits of rock erupt with great force. However, volcanoes begin deep within the earth.

Using the third person makes the passage more formal as well as more authoritative. Short and simple sentences are replaced with longer, more complex sentences, which make the passage more interesting to read. The vocabulary that is used is more sophisticated. Errors in grammar are also corrected. The final result is a text that is informed, precise and finely crafted.

Having an effective conclusion

Equally important to the beginning of an essay is an effective conclusion. A good concluding statement should review and sum up the information or explanation that precedes it in the text so that the reader can feel a sense of closure and completion. The conclusion should flow out of the information and bring the text to a logical end. Ideally the conclusion would review the most important points made in the presentation, the reasoning that is employed, and any supporting details that need to be remembered. A good conclusion should also allow the reader to reflect on what has been said, hopefully in a favorable light.

Narratives

Establishing a context

When writing a narrative, a context for the story has to be introduced; that context could consist of a description of a situation or a setting. A point of view also has to be established. It could be introduced by a narrator and may or may not be the same as the author's. The points of view can be shown through dialogue or how the narrator reacts to or describes what characters do in the story. The characters will need to be drawn very clearly through their descriptions, what they do, and what they say. The author may hide his point of view in the characters' thoughts or actions. The narrator's point of view is usually more overtly seen in what is said in the narrative by the narrator.

Decide the character and point of view in the following passage:

> Alma Way stared straight ahead. Her long delicate face was pale. Her gloved hands, clutching the hymn book, trembled as she sang. The time for her solo was near. She felt panic rising within her but she took a deep breath. Then her voice rang out, clear as a bell. The congregation nodded admiringly.

The author has chosen to tell the narrative from the third-person omniscient viewpoint, which means the narrator is all-knowing. He introduces the character of Alma Way by describing her. He tells the reader a lot about her by describing how she is staring, that her face is pale and that her gloved hands clutched a hymn book. The narrator also tells us that she feels panic. The author has drawn a thorough picture of this woman for whom he seems to have some interest in. The reader would need to read on to learn more clues about what the narrator's and author's viewpoints are.

Sequence of events

The sequence of events in a narrative should follow naturally out of the action and the plot. Rather than being forced, the sequence should follow the natural flow of a dialogue or plot and enhance what happens in the story. The only time that sequence is not in the order that events happens is when an author decides to use the literary device called flashback. In this case the action does not flow in sequence but rather jumps back and forth in time. Events in a narrative are extremely important in helping the reader understand the intent or message of a narrative, which is why it is important to take note of the way in which the plot unfolds.

Techniques used by an author

Authors employ many techniques to make their narratives come alive and have meaning. Dialogue is an important one. It is often through the dialogue that a reader learns what is happening and what a character is like or is thinking. An analysis by the reader of the dialogue can yield important information about what is happening in the narrative. Equally important are the descriptions that an author uses to help the reader visualize a setting and what a character looks or acts like. Another important technique is pacing, which sets the stage for what is happening in a plot, whether the pace is slow and then quick. The pace is the rhythm of the story and can have a strong effect on creating tension in the story,

Transitions words

Transition words are important when writing a narrative so that the reader can follow the events in a seamless manner. They can also color the plot and the characters and show the relationships between experiences and events. Sequence words such as "first," "second," and "last" assist the reader in understanding the order in which events occur, which can be important to the flow of the plot. Words such as "then" or "next" also show the order in which events occur. "After a while" and "before this" are other sequence expressions. Transition words can indicate a change from one time frame or setting to another. "We were sitting on a rock near the lake when we heard a strange sound." At this point we decided to look to see where the noise was coming from by going further into the woods." In this excerpt the phrase "as this point" signals a shift in setting. It also shows the relationship between what was happening and what came next.

Using precise language

An author's precise language can help a reader gain insight into a story that an author has written. Precise language, including phrases and sensory language, helps the reader imagine a place, situation, or person in the way that the writer wishes. The details that an author uses to describe a setting or character will help bring a story to life and convey exactly what the author envisions. Details of what characters do, the setting, and the events in a narrative help create a lively and thought-provoking story. Sensory language helps convey the mood and feeling of the setting and characters and will bring insight into the theme of a narrative. When reading, take special care to understand the range of language that an author employs in order to better comprehend the meaning.

Read the excerpt and analyze its language:

> All through his boyhood, George Willard had been in the habit of walking on Trunion Pike. He had been there on winter nights when it was covered with snow and only the moon looked down at him; he had been there in the fall when bleak winds blew and on summer evenings when the air vibrated with the song of insects.

This excerpt is filled with precise and sensory language. The descriptions of walking on Turnion Pike "when it was covered with snow and only the moon looked down," of the "bleak winds" that blew and times that "the air vibrated with the song of insects" all contribute to bring the writing to life and allowing the reader to see what the author envisions in his mind by creating images through vivid and precise language. The description of the setting uses relevant details that help the reader understand something about George Willard. The language has the effects of drawing the reader into the story and revealing more about this character.

Role of a conclusion

The conclusion of a narrative is extremely important because it shapes the entire story and creates the theme that the author was attempting to convey. The conclusion of a narrative is the resolution of the problem that is faced by the characters. Some conclusions may be tragic, such as those in the many classic tragedies; other endings may be lighthearted, much in the style of classic comedies. Modern stories tend to have endings that are more complex than the clear-cut endings of classic literature. They often leave the reader without a clear sense of how a character fares at the end. Nonetheless, this element tells the reader that life is not always clear in its conclusions, which is a lesson that many writers strive to teach.

Betsy is writing a story about a girl who wants to be on the basketball team and works out every day to get in shape. She has written about the girl's feelings and the obstacles she has had to overcome. Now she wants to find a conclusion to the story. Describe what she should look for when trying to develop a good conclusion.

Betsy should think about her character as though she were a real person because this seems to be a realistic story. She should think about what she wants to have as the story's theme. Does she want to show that hard work pays off? Or does she want to show that you cannot always get what you want even with hard work? In other words, she has to decide whether the story will have a happy ending or not. Whatever kind of an ending she decides upon, the conclusion should bring the entire story to a fitting and appropriate end so that the reader has a sense of closure. It should follow the opening and the many events that happen so that there is a form to the story.

Practice Test

Composition Prompt - Expository Composition

Choose a current social problem about which you feel strongly. How would you resolve this social issue? Identify a specific potential solution and explain your solution in a well-developed essay.

Sample Composition #1 – Expository Composition:

Triumph Through Training Programs

In our current economy, unemployment is a pressing issue. The unemployment numbers for young people, however, are up to 50 percent higher than those for experienced workers. Most young people are not adequately equipped to compete in the work world. This problem can be tackled through training programs designed to help young workers identify their interests, develop skills, and build a professional network.

First, training programs can help unemployed young people identify their interests. Many young workers are clueless about their professional passions and natural aptitudes. Training programs can help them identify these things and find areas in which they should develop. This will help young and inexperienced workers develop passion and motivation for their job search.

Once interests have been identified, training programs can help young workers develop skills in those areas of interest. More practical and focused than college courses, training programs can hone in on specific traits and abilities necessary for particular jobs or industries. Developing these skills can give young workers both confidence and a competitive edge over other job candidates.

With a list of interests and a wealth of new skills, young workers can also use training programs to build a professional network. Industry contacts are more necessary than ever before when conducting a job search. The old adage, "It's not what you know; it's who you know," has proven true for many job seekers. Training programs can help young workers build a professional network of contacts through special speakers, job fairs, internships, and other avenues.

Searching for a job is always daunting, but it can be especially intimidating for workers with little or no experience. Training programs can help ease these fears. They can help workers identify interests, develop skills, and build a professional network of contacts. With these tools—gained through training programs—young workers will be equipped to beat the unemployment obstacles and go out and find the job of their dreams.

General Strategies

The most important thing you can do is to ignore your fears and jump into the test immediately. Do not be overwhelmed by any strange-sounding terms. You have to jump into the test like jumping into a pool—all at once is the easiest way.

Make Predictions

As you read and understand the question, try to guess what the answer will be. Remember that several of the answer choices are wrong, and once you begin reading them, your mind will immediately become cluttered with answer choices designed to throw you off. Your mind is typically the most focused immediately after you have read the question and digested its contents. If you can, try to predict what the correct answer will be. You may be surprised at what you can predict.

Quickly scan the choices and see if your prediction is in the listed answer choices. If it is, then you can be quite confident that you have the right answer. It still won't hurt to check the other answer choices, but most of the time, you've got it!

Answer the Question

It may seem obvious to only pick answer choices that answer the question, but the test writers can create some excellent answer choices that are wrong. Don't pick an answer just because it sounds right, or you believe it to be true. It MUST answer the question. Once you've made your selection, always go back and check it against the question and make sure that you didn't misread the question and that the answer choice does answer the question posed.

Benchmark

After you read the first answer choice, decide if you think it sounds correct or not. If it doesn't, move on to the next answer choice. If it does, mentally mark that answer choice. This doesn't mean that you've definitely selected it as your answer choice, it just means that it's the best you've seen thus far. Go ahead and read the next choice. If the next choice is worse than the one you've already selected, keep going to the next answer choice. If the next choice is better than the choice you've already selected, mentally mark the new answer choice as your best guess.

The first answer choice that you select becomes your standard. Every other answer choice must be benchmarked against that standard. That choice is correct until proven otherwise by another answer choice beating it out. Once you've decided that no other answer choice seems as good, do one final check to ensure that your answer choice answers the question posed.

Valid Information

Don't discount any of the information provided in the question. Every piece of information may be necessary to determine the correct answer. None of the information in the question is there to throw you off (while the answer choices will certainly have information to throw you off). If two seemingly unrelated topics are discussed, don't ignore either. You can be confident there is a relationship, or it wouldn't be included in the question, and you are probably going to have to determine what is that relationship to find the answer.

Avoid "Fact Traps"

Don't get distracted by a choice that is factually true. Your search is for the answer that answers the question. Stay focused and don't fall for an answer that is true but irrelevant. Always go back to the question and make sure you're choosing an answer that actually answers the question and is not just a true statement. An answer can be factually correct, but it MUST answer the question asked. Additionally, two answers can both be seemingly correct, so be sure to read all of the answer choices, and make sure that you get the one that BEST answers the question.

Milk the Question

Some of the questions may throw you completely off. They might deal with a subject you have not been exposed to, or one that you haven't reviewed in years. While your lack of knowledge about the subject will be a hindrance, the question itself can give you many clues that will help you find the correct answer. Read the question carefully and look for clues. Watch particularly for adjectives and nouns describing difficult terms or words that you don't recognize. Regardless of whether you completely understand a word or not, replacing it with a synonym, either provided or one you more familiar with, may help you to understand what the questions are asking. Rather than wracking your mind about specific detailed information concerning a difficult term or word, try to use mental substitutes that are easier to understand.

The Trap of Familiarity

Don't just choose a word because you recognize it. On difficult questions, you may not recognize a number of words in the answer choices. The test writers don't put "make-believe" words on the test, so don't think that just because you only recognize all the words in one answer choice that that answer choice must be correct. If you only recognize words in one answer choice, then focus on that one. Is it correct? Try your best to determine if it is correct. If it is, that's great. If not, eliminate it. Each word and answer choice you eliminate increases your chances of getting the question correct, even if you then have to guess among the unfamiliar choices.

Eliminate Answers

Eliminate choices as soon as you realize they are wrong. But be careful! Make sure you consider all of the possible answer choices. Just because one appears right, doesn't mean that the next one won't be even better! The test writers will usually put more than one good answer choice for every question, so read all of them. Don't worry if you are stuck between two that seem right. By getting down to just two remaining possible choices, your odds are now 50/50. Rather than wasting too much time, play the odds. You are guessing, but guessing wisely because you've been able to knock out some of the answer choices that you know are wrong. If you are eliminating choices and realize that the last answer choice you are left with is also obviously wrong, don't panic. Start over and consider each choice again. There may easily be something that you missed the first time and will realize on the second pass.

Tough Questions

If you are stumped on a problem or it appears too hard or too difficult, don't waste time. Move on! Remember though, if you can quickly check for obviously incorrect answer choices, your chances of guessing correctly are greatly improved. Before you completely give up, at least try to knock out a couple of possible answers. Eliminate what you can and then guess at the remaining answer choices before moving on.

Brainstorm

If you get stuck on a difficult question, spend a few seconds quickly brainstorming. Run through the complete list of possible answer choices. Look at each choice and ask yourself, "Could this answer the question satisfactorily?" Go through each answer choice and consider it independently of the others. By systematically going through all possibilities, you may find something that you would otherwise overlook. Remember though that when you get stuck, it's important to try to keep moving.

Read Carefully

Understand the problem. Read the question and answer choices carefully. Don't miss the question because you misread the terms. You have plenty of time to read each question thoroughly and make sure you understand what is being asked. Yet a happy medium must be attained, so don't waste too much time. You must read carefully, but efficiently.

Face Value

When in doubt, use common sense. Always accept the situation in the problem at face value. Don't read too much into it. These problems will not require you to make huge leaps of logic. The test writers aren't trying to throw you off with a cheap trick. If you have to go beyond creativity and make a leap of logic in order to have an answer choice answer the question, then you should look at the other answer choices. Don't overcomplicate the problem by creating theoretical relationships or explanations that will warp time or space. These are normal problems rooted in reality. It's just that the applicable relationship or explanation may not be readily apparent and you have to figure things out. Use your common sense to interpret anything that isn't clear.

Prefixes

If you're having trouble with a word in the question or answer choices, try dissecting it. Take advantage of every clue that the word might include. Prefixes and suffixes can be a huge help. Usually they allow you to determine a basic meaning. Pre- means before, post- means after, pro - is positive, de- is negative. From these prefixes and suffixes, you can get an idea of the general meaning of the word and try to put it into context. Beware though of any traps. Just because con- is the opposite of pro-, doesn't necessarily mean congress is the opposite of progress!

Hedge Phrases

Watch out for critical hedge phrases, led off with words such as "likely," "may," "can," "sometimes," "often," "almost," "mostly," "usually," "generally," "rarely," and "sometimes." Question writers insert these hedge phrases to cover every possibility. Often an answer choice will be wrong simply because it leaves no room for exception. Unless the situation calls for them, avoid answer choices that have definitive words like "exactly," and "always."

Switchback Words

Stay alert for "switchbacks." These are the words and phrases frequently used to alert you to shifts in thought. The most common switchback word is "but." Others include "although," "however," "nevertheless," "on the other hand," "even though," "while," "in spite of," "despite," and "regardless of."

New Information

Correct answer choices will rarely have completely new information included. Answer choices typically are straightforward reflections of the material asked about and will directly relate to the question. If a new piece of information is included in an answer choice that doesn't even seem to relate to the topic being asked about, then that answer choice is likely incorrect. All of the information needed to answer the question is usually provided for you in the question. You should not have to make guesses that are unsupported or choose answer choices that require unknown information that cannot be reasoned from what is given.

Time Management

On technical questions, don't get lost on the technical terms. Don't spend too much time on any one question. If you don't know what a term means, then odds are you aren't going to get much further since you don't have a dictionary. You should be able to immediately recognize whether or not you know a term. If you don't, work with the other clues that you have—the other answer choices and terms provided—but don't waste too much time trying to figure out a difficult term that you don't know.

Contextual Clues

Look for contextual clues. An answer can be right but not the correct answer. The contextual clues will help you find the answer that is most right and is correct. Understand the context in which a phrase or statement is made. This will help you make important distinctions.

Don't Panic

Panicking will not answer any questions for you; therefore, it isn't helpful. When you first see the question, if your mind goes blank, take a deep breath. Force yourself to mechanically go through the steps of solving the problem using the strategies you've learned.

Pace Yourself

Don't get clock fever. It's easy to be overwhelmed when you're looking at a page full of questions, your mind is full of random thoughts and feeling confused, and the clock is ticking down faster than you would like. Calm down and maintain the pace that you have set for yourself. As long as you are on track by monitoring your pace, you are guaranteed to have enough time for yourself. When you get to the last few minutes of the test, it may seem like you won't have enough time left, but if you only have as many questions as you should have left at that point, then you're right on track!

Answer Selection

The best way to pick an answer choice is to eliminate all of those that are wrong, until only one is left and confirm that is the correct answer. Sometimes though, an answer choice may immediately look right. Be careful! Take a second to make sure that the other choices are not equally obvious. Don't make a hasty mistake. There are only two times that you should stop before checking other answers. First is when you are positive that the answer choice you have selected is correct. Second is when time is almost out and you have to make a quick guess!

Check Your Work

Since you will probably not know every term listed and the answer to every question, it is important that you get credit for the ones that you do know. Don't miss any questions through careless mistakes. If at all possible, try to take a second to look back over your answer selection and make sure you've selected the correct answer choice and haven't made a costly careless mistake (such as marking an answer choice that you didn't mean to mark). The time it takes for this quick double check should more than pay for itself in caught mistakes.

Beware of Directly Quoted Answers

Sometimes an answer choice will repeat word for word a portion of the question or reference section. However, beware of such exact duplication. It may be a trap! More than likely, the correct choice will paraphrase or summarize a point, rather than being exactly the same wording.

Slang

Scientific sounding answers are better than slang ones. An answer choice that begins "To compare the outcomes..." is much more likely to be correct than one that begins "Because some people insisted..."

Extreme Statements

Avoid wild answers that throw out highly controversial ideas that are proclaimed as established fact. An answer choice that states the "process should used in certain situations, if..." is much more likely to be correct than one that states the "process should be discontinued completely." The first is a calm rational statement and doesn't even make a definitive, uncompromising stance, using a hedge word "if" to provide wiggle room, whereas the second choice is a radical idea and far more extreme.

Answer Choice Families

When you have two or more answer choices that are direct opposites or parallels, one of them is usually the correct answer. For instance, if one answer choice states "x increases" and another answer choice states "x decreases" or "y increases," then those two or three answer choices are very similar in construction and fall into the same family of answer choices. A family of answer choices consists of two or three answer choices, very similar in construction, but often with directly opposite meanings. Usually the correct answer choice will be in that family of answer choices. The "odd man out" or answer choice that doesn't seem to fit the parallel construction of the other answer choices is more likely to be incorrect.

How to Overcome Test Anxiety

The very nature of tests caters to some level of anxiety, nervousness, or tension, just as we feel for any important event that occurs in our lives. A little bit of anxiety or nervousness can be a good thing. It helps us with motivation, and makes achievement just that much sweeter. However, too much anxiety can be a problem, especially if it hinders our ability to function and perform.

"Test anxiety," is the term that refers to the emotional reactions that some test-takers experience when faced with a test or exam. Having a fear of testing and exams is based upon a rational fear, since the test-taker's performance can shape the course of an academic career. Nevertheless, experiencing excessive fear of examinations will only interfere with the test-taker's ability to perform and chance to be successful.

There are a large variety of causes that can contribute to the development and sensation of test anxiety. These include, but are not limited to, lack of preparation and worrying about issues surrounding the test.

Lack of Preparation

Lack of preparation can be identified by the following behaviors or situations:

Not scheduling enough time to study, and therefore cramming the night before the test or exam
Managing time poorly, to create the sensation that there is not enough time to do everything
Failing to organize the text information in advance, so that the study material consists of the entire text and not simply the pertinent information
Poor overall studying habits

Worrying, on the other hand, can be related to both the test taker, or many other factors around him/her that will be affected by the results of the test. These include worrying about:

Previous performances on similar exams, or exams in general
How friends and other students are achieving
The negative consequences that will result from a poor grade or failure

There are three primary elements to test anxiety. Physical components, which involve the same typical bodily reactions as those to acute anxiety (to be discussed below). Emotional factors have to do with fear or panic. Mental or cognitive issues concerning attention spans and memory abilities.

Physical Signals

There are many different symptoms of test anxiety, and these are not limited to mental and emotional strain. Frequently there are a range of physical signals that will let a test taker know that he/she is suffering from test anxiety. These bodily changes can include the following:

Perspiring
Sweaty palms
Wet, trembling hands
Nausea
Dry mouth
A knot in the stomach
Headache
Faintness
Muscle tension
Aching shoulders, back and neck
Rapid heart beat
Feeling too hot/cold

To recognize the sensation of test anxiety, a test-taker should monitor him/herself for the following sensations:

The physical distress symptoms as listed above
Emotional sensitivity, expressing emotional feelings such as the need to cry or laugh too much, or a sensation of anger or helplessness
A decreased ability to think, causing the test-taker to blank out or have racing thoughts that are hard to organize or control.

Though most students will feel some level of anxiety when faced with a test or exam, the majority can cope with that anxiety and maintain it at a manageable level. However, those who cannot are faced with a very real and very serious condition, which can and should be controlled for the immeasurable benefit of this sufferer.

Naturally, these sensations lead to negative results for the testing experience. The most common effects of test anxiety have to do with nervousness and mental blocking.

Nervousness

Nervousness can appear in several different levels:

The test-taker's difficulty, or even inability to read and understand the questions on the test
The difficulty or inability to organize thoughts to a coherent form
The difficulty or inability to recall key words and concepts relating to the testing questions (especially essays)
The receipt of poor grades on a test, though the test material was well known by the test taker

Conversely, a person may also experience mental blocking, which involves:

Blanking out on test questions
Only remembering the correct answers to the questions when the test has already finished.

Fortunately for test anxiety sufferers, beating these feelings, to a large degree, has to do with proper preparation. When a test taker has a feeling of preparedness, then anxiety will be dramatically lessened.

The first step to resolving anxiety issues is to distinguish which of the two types of anxiety are being suffered. If the anxiety is a direct result of a lack of preparation, this should be considered a normal reaction, and the anxiety level (as opposed to the test results) shouldn't be anything to worry about. However, if, when adequately prepared, the test-taker still panics, blanks out, or seems to overreact, this is not a fully rational reaction. While this can be considered normal too, there are many ways to combat and overcome these effects.

Remember that anxiety cannot be entirely eliminated, however, there are ways to minimize it, to make the anxiety easier to manage. Preparation is one of the best ways to minimize test anxiety. Therefore the following techniques are wise in order to best fight off any anxiety that may want to build.

To begin with, try to avoid cramming before a test, whenever it is possible. By trying to memorize an entire term's worth of information in one day, you'll be shocking your system, and not giving yourself a very good chance to absorb the information. This is an easy path to anxiety, so for those who suffer from test anxiety, cramming should not even be considered an option.

Instead of cramming, work throughout the semester to combine all of the material which is presented throughout the semester, and work on it gradually as the course goes by, making sure to master the main concepts first, leaving minor details for a week or so before the test.

To study for the upcoming exam, be sure to pose questions that may be on the examination, to gauge the ability to answer them by integrating the ideas from your texts, notes and lectures, as well as any supplementary readings.

If it is truly impossible to cover all of the information that was covered in that particular term, concentrate on the most important portions, that can be covered very well. Learn these concepts as best as possible, so that when the test comes, a goal can be made to use these concepts as presentations of your knowledge.

In addition to study habits, changes in attitude are critical to beating a struggle with test anxiety. In fact, an improvement of the perspective over the entire test-taking experience can actually help a test taker to enjoy studying and therefore improve the overall experience. Be certain not to overemphasize the significance of the grade - know that the result of the test is neither a reflection of self worth, nor is it a measure of intelligence; one grade will not predict a person's future success.
To improve an overall testing outlook, the following steps should be tried:

Keeping in mind that the most reasonable expectation for taking a test is to expect to try to demonstrate as much of what you know as you possibly can.
Reminding ourselves that a test is only one test; this is not the only one, and there will be others.
The thought of thinking of oneself in an irrational, all-or-nothing term should be avoided at all costs.

A reward should be designated for after the test, so there's something to look forward to. Whether it be going to a movie, going out to eat, or simply visiting friends, schedule it in advance, and do it no matter what result is expected on the exam.

Test-takers should also keep in mind that the basics are some of the most important things, even beyond anti-anxiety techniques and studying. Never neglect the basic social, emotional and biological needs, in order to try to absorb information. In order to best achieve, these three factors must be held as just as important as the studying itself.

Study Steps

Remember the following important steps for studying:

Maintain healthy nutrition and exercise habits. Continue both your recreational activities and social pass times. These both contribute to your physical and emotional well being. Be certain to get a good amount of sleep, especially the night before the test, because when you're overtired you are not able to perform to the best of your best ability.
Keep the studying pace to a moderate level by taking breaks when they are needed, and varying the work whenever possible, to keep the mind fresh instead of getting bored. When enough studying has been done that all the material that can be learned has been learned, and the test taker is prepared for the test, stop studying and do something relaxing such as listening to music, watching a movie, or taking a warm bubble bath.

There are also many other techniques to minimize the uneasiness or apprehension that is experienced along with test anxiety before, during, or even after the examination. In fact, there are a great deal of things that can be done to stop anxiety from interfering with lifestyle and performance. Again, remember that anxiety will not be eliminated entirely, and it shouldn't be. Otherwise that "up" feeling for exams would not exist, and most of us depend on that sensation to perform better than usual. However, this anxiety has to be at a level that is manageable.

Of course, as we have just discussed, being prepared for the exam is half the battle right away. Attending all classes, finding out what knowledge will be expected on the exam, and knowing the exam schedules are easy steps to lowering anxiety. Keeping up with work will remove the need to cram, and efficient study habits will eliminate wasted time. Studying should be done in an ideal location for concentration, so that it is simple to become interested in the material and give it complete attention. A method such as SQ3R (Survey, Question, Read, Recite, Review) is a wonderful key to follow to make sure that the study habits are as effective as possible, especially in the case of learning from a textbook. Flashcards are great techniques for memorization. Learning to take good notes will mean that notes will be full of useful information, so that less sifting will need to be done to seek out what is pertinent for studying. Reviewing notes after class and then again on occasion will keep the information fresh in the mind. From notes that have been taken summary sheets and outlines can be made for simpler reviewing.

A study group can also be a very motivational and helpful place to study, as there will be a sharing of ideas, all of the minds can work together, to make sure that everyone understands, and the studying will be made more interesting because it will be a social occasion.

Basically, though, as long as the test-taker remains organized and self confident, with efficient study habits, less time will need to be spent studying, and higher grades will be achieved.

To become self confident, there are many useful steps. The first of these is "self talk." It has been shown through extensive research, that self-talk for students who suffer from test anxiety, should be well monitored, in order to make sure that it contributes to self confidence as opposed to sinking the student. Frequently the self talk of test-anxious students is negative or self-defeating, thinking that everyone else is smarter and faster, that they always mess up, and that if they don't do well, they'll fail the entire course. It is important to decreasing anxiety that awareness is made of self talk. Try writing any negative self thoughts and then disputing them with a positive statement instead. Begin self-encouragement as though it was a friend speaking. Repeat positive statements to help reprogram the mind to believing in successes instead of failures.

Helpful Techniques

Other extremely helpful techniques include:

Self-visualization of doing well and reaching goals
While aiming for an "A" level of understanding, don't try to "overprotect" by setting your expectations lower. This will only convince the mind to stop studying in order to meet the lower expectations.
Don't make comparisons with the results or habits of other students. These are individual factors, and different things work for different people, causing different results.
Strive to become an expert in learning what works well, and what can be done in order to improve. Consider collecting this data in a journal.
Create rewards for after studying instead of doing things before studying that will only turn into avoidance behaviors.
Make a practice of relaxing - by using methods such as progressive relaxation, self-hypnosis, guided imagery, etc - in order to make relaxation an automatic sensation.
Work on creating a state of relaxed concentration so that concentrating will take on the focus of the mind, so that none will be wasted on worrying.
Take good care of the physical self by eating well and getting enough sleep.
Plan in time for exercise and stick to this plan.

Beyond these techniques, there are other methods to be used before, during and after the test that will help the test-taker perform well in addition to overcoming anxiety.

Before the exam comes the academic preparation. This involves establishing a study schedule and beginning at least one week before the actual date of the test. By doing this, the anxiety of not having enough time to study for the test will be automatically eliminated. Moreover, this will make the studying a much more effective experience, ensuring that the learning will be an easier process. This relieves much undue pressure on the test-taker.

Summary sheets, note cards, and flash cards with the main concepts and examples of these main concepts should be prepared in advance of the actual studying time. A topic should never be eliminated from this process. By omitting a topic because it isn't expected to be on the test is only setting up the test-taker for anxiety should it actually appear on the exam. Utilize the course syllabus for laying out the topics that should be studied. Carefully go over the notes that were made in class, paying special attention to any of the issues that the professor took special care to emphasize while lecturing in class. In the textbooks, use the chapter review, or if possible, the chapter tests, to begin your review.

It may even be possible to ask the instructor what information will be covered on the exam, or what the format of the exam will be (for example, multiple choice, essay, free form, true-false). Additionally, see if it is possible to find out how many questions will be on the test. If a review sheet or sample test has been offered by the professor, make good use of it, above anything else, for the preparation for the test. Another great resource for getting to know the examination is reviewing tests from previous semesters. Use these tests to review, and aim to achieve a 100% score on each of the possible topics. With a few exceptions, the goal that you set for yourself is the highest one that you will reach.

Take all of the questions that were assigned as homework, and rework them to any other possible course material. The more problems reworked, the more skill and confidence will form as a result. When forming the solution to a problem, write out each of the steps. Don't simply do head work. By doing as many steps on paper as possible, much clarification and therefore confidence will be formed. Do this with as many homework problems as possible, before checking the answers. By checking the answer after each problem, a reinforcement will exist, that will not be on the exam. Study situations should be as exam-like as possible, to prime the test-taker's system for the experience. By waiting to check the answers at the end, a psychological advantage will be formed, to decrease the stress factor.

Another fantastic reason for not cramming is the avoidance of confusion in concepts, especially when it comes to mathematics. 8-10 hours of study will become one hundred percent more effective if it is spread out over a week or at least several days, instead of doing it all in one sitting. Recognize that the human brain requires time in order to assimilate new material, so frequent breaks and a span of study time over several days will be much more beneficial.

Additionally, don't study right up until the point of the exam. Studying should stop a minimum of one hour before the exam begins. This allows the brain to rest and put things in their proper order. This will also provide the time to become as relaxed as possible when going into the examination room. The test-taker will also have time to eat well and eat sensibly. Know that the brain needs food as much as the rest of the body. With enough food and enough sleep, as well as a relaxed attitude, the body and the mind are primed for success.

Avoid any anxious classmates who are talking about the exam. These students only spread anxiety, and are not worth sharing the anxious sentimentalities.

Before the test also involves creating a positive attitude, so mental preparation should also be a point of concentration. There are many keys to creating a positive attitude. Should fears become rushing in, make a visualization of taking the exam, doing well, and seeing an A written on the paper. Write out a list of affirmations that will bring a feeling of confidence, such as "I am doing well in my English class," "I studied well and know my material," "I enjoy this class." Even if the affirmations aren't believed at first, it sends a positive message to the subconscious which will result in an alteration of the overall belief system, which is the system that creates reality.

If a sensation of panic begins, work with the fear and imagine the very worst! Work through the entire scenario of not passing the test, failing the entire course, and dropping out of school, followed by not getting a job, and pushing a shopping cart through the dark alley where you'll live. This will place things into perspective! Then, practice deep breathing and create a visualization of the opposite situation - achieving an "A" on the exam, passing the entire course, receiving the degree at a graduation ceremony.

On the day of the test, there are many things to be done to ensure the best results, as well as the most calm outlook. The following stages are suggested in order to maximize test-taking potential:

Begin the examination day with a moderate breakfast, and avoid any coffee or beverages with caffeine if the test taker is prone to jitters. Even people who are used to managing caffeine can feel jittery or light-headed when it is taken on a test day.
Attempt to do something that is relaxing before the examination begins. As last minute cramming clouds the mastering of overall concepts, it is better to use this time to create a calming outlook.
Be certain to arrive at the test location well in advance, in order to provide time to select a location that is away from doors, windows and other distractions, as well as giving enough time to relax before the test begins.
Keep away from anxiety generating classmates who will upset the sensation of stability and relaxation that is being attempted before the exam.
Should the waiting period before the exam begins cause anxiety, create a self-distraction by reading a light magazine or something else that is relaxing and simple.

During the exam itself, read the entire exam from beginning to end, and find out how much time should be allotted to each individual problem. Once writing the exam, should more time be taken for a problem, it should be abandoned, in order to begin another problem. If there is time at the end, the unfinished problem can always be returned to and completed.

Read the instructions very carefully - twice - so that unpleasant surprises won't follow during or after the exam has ended.

When writing the exam, pretend that the situation is actually simply the completion of homework within a library, or at home. This will assist in forming a relaxed atmosphere, and will allow the brain extra focus for the complex thinking function.

Begin the exam with all of the questions with which the most confidence is felt. This will build the confidence level regarding the entire exam and will begin a quality momentum. This will also create encouragement for trying the problems where uncertainty resides.

Going with the "gut instinct" is always the way to go when solving a problem. Second guessing should be avoided at all costs. Have confidence in the ability to do well.

For essay questions, create an outline in advance that will keep the mind organized and make certain that all of the points are remembered. For multiple choice, read every answer, even if the correct one has been spotted - a better one may exist.

Continue at a pace that is reasonable and not rushed, in order to be able to work carefully. Provide enough time to go over the answers at the end, to check for small errors that can be corrected.

Should a feeling of panic begin, breathe deeply, and think of the feeling of the body releasing sand through its pores. Visualize a calm, peaceful place, and include all of the sights, sounds and sensations of this image. Continue the deep breathing, and take a few minutes to continue this with closed eyes. When all is well again, return to the test.

If a "blanking" occurs for a certain question, skip it and move on to the next question. There will be time to return to the other question later. Get everything done that can be done, first, to guarantee all the grades that can be compiled, and to build all of the confidence possible. Then return to the weaker questions to build the marks from there.

Remember, one's own reality can be created, so as long as the belief is there, success will follow. And remember: anxiety can happen later, right now, there's an exam to be written!

After the examination is complete, whether there is a feeling for a good grade or a bad grade, don't dwell on the exam, and be certain to follow through on the reward that was promised...and enjoy it! Don't dwell on any mistakes that have been made, as there is nothing that can be done at this point anyway.

Additionally, don't begin to study for the next test right away. Do something relaxing for a while, and let the mind relax and prepare itself to begin absorbing information again.

From the results of the exam - both the grade and the entire experience, be certain to learn from what has gone on. Perfect studying habits and work some more on confidence in order to make the next examination experience even better than the last one.

Learn to avoid places where openings occurred for laziness, procrastination and day dreaming.

Use the time between this exam and the next one to better learn to relax, even learning to relax on cue, so that any anxiety can be controlled during the next exam. Learn how to relax the body. Slouch in your chair if that helps. Tighten and then relax all of the different muscle groups, one group at a time, beginning with the feet and then working all the way up to the neck and face. This will ultimately relax the muscles more than they were to begin with. Learn how to breathe deeply and comfortably, and focus on this breathing going in and out as a relaxing thought. With every exhale, repeat the word "relax."

As common as test anxiety is, it is very possible to overcome it. Make yourself one of the test-takers who overcome this frustrating hindrance.

Additional Bonus Material

Due to our efforts to try to keep this book to a manageable length, we've created a link that will give you access to all of your additional bonus material.

Please visit http://www.mometrix.com/bonus948/actaspireg8 to access the information.